Ninth Edition

Sentence Skills
A Workbook for Writers

Ninth Edition

Sentence Skills
A Workbook for Writers

John Langan
Atlantic Cape Community College

Connect
Learn
Succeed™

The McGraw·Hill Companies

Connect
Learn
Succeed™

SENTENCE SKILLS: A WORKBOOK FOR WRITERS, NINTH EDITION

Published by McGraw-Hill, a business unit of The McGraw-Hill Companies, Inc., 1221 Avenue of the Amerias, New York, NY 10020. Copyright © 2011 by The McGraw-Hill Companies, Inc. All rights reserved. Previous editions © 2008, 2003, and 1999. No part of this publication may be reproduced or distributed in any form or by any means, or stored in a database or retrieval system, without the prior written consent of The McGraw-Hill Companies, Inc., including, but not limited to, in any network or other electronic storage or transmission, or broadcast for distance learning.

Some ancillaries, including electronic and print components, may not be available to customers outside the United States.

This book is printed on acid-free paper.

2 3 4 5 6 7 8 9 0 DOC/DOC 1 0 9 8 7 6 5 4 3 2 1

ISBN: 978-0-07-337169-6
MHID: 0-07-337169-6 (Student's Edition)
ISBN: 978-0-07-735374-2
MHID: 0-07-735374-9 (Instructor's Edition)

Vice President & Editor-in-Chief: *Michael Ryan*
Vice President EDP/Central Publishing Services:
  Kimberly Meriwether David
Publisher: *David Patterson*
Senior Sponsoring Editor: *John Kindler*
Executive Marketing Manager: *Pamela S. Cooper*
Editorial Coordinator: *Marley Magaziner*
Project Manager: *Robin A. Reed*
Design Coordinator: *Margarite Reynolds*

Lead Photo Editor: *Alexandra Ambrose*
Cover Images: *Laptop: © Tim Hawley/Getty Images; Pencils: © Nicholas Monu/iStock; Phone: © iStock; Notebook: © Stockbyte/Getty Images*
Buyer: *Laura Fuller*
Media Project Manager: *Sridevi Palani*
Compositor: *Aptara®, Inc.*
Typeface: *11/13 Times*
Printer: *R.R. Donnelley*

All credits appearing on page or at the end of the book are considered to be an extension of the copyright page.

Library of Congress Cataloging-in-Publication Data

Langan, John, 1942–
    Sentence skills : a workbook for writers: form A / John Langan.—9th ed.
        p. cm.
"Annotated Instructor's Edition."
Includes index.
ISBN-13: 978-0-07-735374-2 (Instructor's bk.: alk. paper)
ISBN-10: 0-07-735374-9 (Instructor's bk.: alk. paper)
ISBN-13: 978-0-07-337169-6 (Student's bk.: alk. paper)
ISBN-10: 0-07-337169-6 (Student's bk.: alk paper)
1. English language—Sentences—Problems, exercises, etc. 2. English language—Grammar—Problems, exercises, etc.   I. Title.
PE1441.L352 2010
808'.042076—dc22

2010004824

www.mhhe.com

Praise for *Sentence Skills*

"Clear grammar explanations are the greatest strength of this book. The explanations are easy for students to digest."
—Janice Heigis, Northern Virginia Community College

"Sentence Skills not only presents the concepts well, it offers ample engaging practice opportunities, creating the repetition necessary for student retention of those concepts."
—Michelle Abbott, Georgia Highlands College

"The exercises are plentiful and useful. I particularly like the way that each chapter provides exercises on each subtopic and then mixes subtopics together in a Review Test."
—Jessica Rabin, Anne Arundel Community College

"I can say without reservation that I am impressed with this text, and I would certainly recommend it to colleagues."
—Milton Bentley, Central Georgia Technical College

"The major strengths of this book are its readability, its accuracy, and its completeness. It may be the best of its type."
—Dennis Tettelbach, Georgia Perimeter College

"The book is well organized, concise, and comprehensive. Sentence Skills is not just for this one course. It is a great reference book. I encourage my students to keep it and refer back to it when any question about basic concepts in English arises."
—Stephanie Bechtel Gooding, University of Maryland, University College-Europe

"The Langan books truly provide the clearest explanations of grammar rules."
—Lisa Moreno, Los Angeles Trade Technical College

About the Author

John Langan has taught and authored books on writing and reading skills for over thirty years. Before teaching, he earned advanced degrees in writing at Rutgers University and in reading at Rowan University. John now lives with his wife, Judith Nadell, near Philadelphia. In addition to his wife and Philly sports teams, his passions include reading and turning nonreaders on to the pleasure and power of books. Through Townsend Press, his educational publishing company, he has developed the nonprofit "Townsend Library"—a collection of more than a hundred new and classic stories with wide appeal to readers of all ages.

Contents

PART 3   Reinforcement of the Skills   452

APPENDIXES   514

Key Features of the Book

Sentence Skills will help students learn to write effectively. It is an all-in-one text that includes a basic rhetoric and gives full attention to grammar, punctuation, mechanics, and usage.

The book contains eight distinctive features to aid instructors and their students:

1. **Coverage of basic writing skills is exceptionally thorough.**

   The book pays special attention to fragments, run-ons, verbs, and other areas where students have serious problems. At the same time, a glance at the table of contents shows that the book treats skills (such as dictionary use and spelling improvement) not found in most other texts. In addition, parts of the book are devoted to the basics of effective writing, to practice in editing and proofreading, and to achieving variety in sentences.

2. **The book has a clear and flexible format.**

   It is organized in three easy-to-use parts. Part One is a guide to the goals of effective writing followed by a series of activities to help students practice and master those goals. Part Two is a comprehensive treatment of the rules of grammar, mechanics, punctuation, and usage needed for clear writing. Part Three provides a series of combined mastery, editing, and proofreading tests to reinforce the sentence skills presented in Part Two.

   Because parts, sections, and chapters are self-contained, instructors can move easily from, for instance, a rhetorical principle in Part One to a grammar rule in Part Two to a combined mastery test in Part Three.

3. **Opening chapters deal with the writer's attitude, writing as a process, and the importance of specific details in writing.**

   In its opening pages, the book helps students recognize and deal with their attitude toward writing—an important part of learning to write well. In the pages that follow, students are encouraged to see writing as a multistage process that moves from prewriting to proofreading. Later, a series of activities helps students understand the nature of specific details and how to generate and use those details. As writing teachers well know, learning to write concretely is a key step for students to master in becoming effective writers.

4. Practice activities are numerous.

Most skills are reinforced by practice activities, review tests, and mastery tests, as well as tests in the *Instructor's Manual.* For many of the skills in the book, there are over one hundred practice sentences.

5. Practice materials are varied and lively.

In many basic writing texts, exercises are monotonous and dry, causing students to lose interest in the skills presented. In *Sentence Skills,* many exercises involve students in various ways. An inductive opening activity allows students to see what they already know about a given skill. Within chapters, students may be asked to underline answers, add words, generate their own sentences, or edit passages. And the lively and engaging practice materials in the book both maintain interest and help students appreciate the value of vigorous details in writing.

6. Active learning strategies appear throughout.

Key chapters of the book feature *collaborative* and *reflective activities* which help make students active participants in their learning. Using group discussion, team writing, and student-generated examples, these activities lend energy to the classroom and strengthen students' mastery of essential writing skills.

7. Terminology is kept to a minimum.

In general, rules are explained using words students already know. A clause is a *word group* having a subject and a verb; a coordinating conjunction is a *joining word;* a nonrestrictive element is an *interrupter.* At the same time, traditional grammatical terms are mentioned briefly for students who learned them somewhere in the past and are comfortable seeing them again.

8. Self-teaching is encouraged.

Students may check their answers to the introductory activities and the practice activities in Part One by referring to the answers in Appendix F. In this way, they are given the responsibility for teaching themselves. At the same time, to ensure that the answer key is used as a learning tool only, answers are *not* given for the review tests in Part Two or for any of the reinforcement tests in Part Three. These answers appear in the *Annotated Instructor's Edition* and the *Instructor's Manual;* they can be copied and handed out to students at the discretion of the instructor.

9. Diagnostic and achievement tests are provided.

These tests appear in Appendixes D and E of the book. Each test may be given in two parts, the second of which provides instructors with a particularly detailed picture of a student's skill level.

Changes to the Ninth Edition

Here are the major changes to this new edition of *Sentence Skills:*

- Writing assignments, review tests, and mastery tests have been thoroughly revised to further reinforce the skills and activities presented in the book.

- Most photographs now include writing prompts to promote critical thinking and get students writing about topics and issues relevant to their lives. In addition, the lively four-color design is bolstered by new part-opening and interior photographs that enhance the book's content and give today's visually oriented students even more help in making connections between thinking and writing.

- Dozens of contemporary items and references have been added to the examples and practice materials so that students see themselves in the pages of the book and can further relate to the material presented.

- The Online Learning Center, which includes instructional aids and resources for both students and instructors, has been thoroughly updated.

Helpful Learning Aids Accompany the Book

Supplements for Instructors

- An *Annotated Instructor's Edition* (ISBN 0-07-735374-9) consists of the student text complete with answers to all activities and tests. Throughout the text, marginal Teaching Tips and ESL Tips offer suggestions for various approaches, classroom activities, discussions, and assignments.

- An *Online Learning Center* (**www.mhhe.com/langan**) offers a host of instructional aids and additional resources for instructors, including a comprehensive Test Bank, an Instructor's Manual, PowerPoint Slides, and more.

Supplements for Students

- An *Online Learning Center* (**www.mhhe.com/langan**) offers a host of study aids and additional resources for students including diagnostic quizzes, a guide to electronic resources, plagiarism and the Internet, a study skills primer, learning styles assessment, and more.

Acknowledgments

Reviewers who have contributed to this edition through their helpful comments include

Janice Heiges, *Northern Virginia Community College*

Michelle Abbott, *Georgia Highlands College*

Jessica Rabin, *Anne Arundel Community College*

Kelly Dedmon, *Isothermal Community College*

I owe thanks as well for the support provided by John Kindler, Marley Magaziner, and Janice Wiggins-Clarke at McGraw-Hill. My gratitude also goes to Paul Langan, who has helped this book become even more student-friendly than it was before.

Joyce Stern, Assistant Professor at Nassau Community College, contributed the ESL Tips to the *Annotated Instructor's Edition* of *Sentence Skills*. Professor Stern is also Assistant to the Chair in the department of Reading and Basic Education. An educator for over thirty years, she holds an advanced degree in TESOL from Hunter College, as well as a New York State Teaching Certificate in TESOL. She is currently coordinating the design, implementation, and recruitment of learning communities for both ESL and developmental students at Nassau Community College and has been recognized by the college's Center for Students with Disabilities for her dedication to student learning.

Donna T. Matsumoto, Assistant Professor of English and the Writing Discipline Coordinator at Leeward Community College in Hawaii (Pearl City), wrote the Teaching Tips for the *Annotated Instructor's Edition* of *Sentence Skills*. Professor Matsumoto has taught writing, women's studies, and American studies for a number of years throughout the University of Hawaii system, at Hawaii Pacific University, and in community schools for adults. She received a 2005 WebCT Exemplary Course Project award for her online writing course and is the author of McGraw-Hill's *The Virtual Workbook,* an online workbook featuring interactive activities and exercises.

John Langan

Ninth Edition

Sentence Skills
A Workbook for Writers

PART 1

Effective Writing

Introduction

Part One is a guide to the goals of effective writing and includes a series of activities to help you practice and master these goals. Begin with the introductory chapter, which makes clear the reasons for learning sentence skills. Then move on to Chapter 2, which presents all the essentials you need to know to become an effective writer. You will be introduced to the four goals of effective writing and will work through a series of activities designed to strengthen your understanding of these goals. Finally, walk through the steps of the writing process—from prewriting to proofreading—in Chapter 3. Examples and activities are provided to illustrate each step, and after completing the activities, you'll be ready to take on the paragraph writing assignments at the end of the chapter.

At the same time that you are writing papers, start working through the sentence skills in Parts Two and Three of the book. Practicing the sentence skills in the context of actual writing assignments is the surest way to master the rules of grammar, mechanics, punctuation, and usage.

Good writing skills are a vital part of almost every career today. The nurse in the above photo, for example, must be able to write clearly and effectively so that others understand the medical needs of her patients. What do you think could happen to a patient if what this nurse has written is difficult to understand because of poor writing skills? Now think about your ideal job and imagine how writing will affect your day-to-day responsibilities. On a separate piece of paper, make a list of ways that effective writing skills will help you on the job.

Learning Sentence Skills

Why Learn Sentence Skills?

Why should someone planning a career as a nurse have to learn sentence skills? Why should an accounting major have to pass a competency test in grammar as part of a college education? Why should a potential physical therapist or graphic artist or computer programmer have to spend hours on the rules of English? Perhaps you are asking questions like these after finding yourself in a class with this book. On the other hand, perhaps you *know* you need to strengthen your basic writing skills, even though you may be unclear about the specific ways the skills will be of use to you. Whatever your views, you should understand why sentence skills—all the rules that make up standard English—are so important.

Clear Communication

Standard English, or "language by the book," is needed to communicate your thoughts to others with a minimal amount of distortion and misinterpretation. Knowing the traditional rules of grammar, punctuation, and usage will help you write clear sentences when communicating with others. You may have heard of the party game in which one person whispers a message to the next person; the message is passed in this way down a line of several other people. By the time the last person in line is asked to give the message aloud, it is usually so garbled and inaccurate that it barely resembles the original. Written communication in some form of English other than standard English carries the same potential for disaster.

To see how important standard English is to written communication, examine the pairs of sentences in the box on the following pages and answer the questions in each case.

1. Which sentence indicates that there might be a plot against Ted?
   a. We should leave Ted. These fumes might be poisonous.
   b. We should leave, Ted. These fumes might be poisonous.

2. Which sentence encourages self-mutilation?
   a. Leave your paper and hand in the dissecting kit.
   b. Leave your paper, and hand in the dissecting kit.

3. Which sentence indicates that the writer has a weak grasp of geography?
   a. As a child, I lived in Lake Worth, which is close to Palm Beach and Alaska.
   b. As a child, I lived in Lake Worth, which is close to Palm Beach, and Alaska.

4. In which sentence does the dog warden seem dangerous?
   a. Foaming at the mouth, the dog warden picked up the stray.
   b. Foaming at the mouth, the stray was picked up by the dog warden.

5. Which announcer was probably fired from the job?
   a. Outside the Academy Awards theater, the announcer called the guests names as they arrived.
   b. Outside the Academy Awards theater, the announcer called the guests' names as they arrived.

6. Below are the opening lines of two students' exam essays. Which student seems likely to earn a higher grade?
   a. Defense mechanisms is the way people hides their inner feelings and deals with stress. There is several types that we use to be protecting our true feelings.
   b. Defense mechanisms are the methods people use to cope with stress. Using a defense mechanism allows a person to hide his or her real desires and goals.

7. The following lines are taken from two English papers. Which student seems likely to earn a higher grade?
   a. A big problem on this campus is apathy, students don't participate in college activities. Such as clubs, student government, and plays.
   b. The most pressing problem on campus is the disgraceful state of the student lounge area. The floor is dirty, the chairs are torn, and the ceiling leaks.

continued

8. The following sentences are taken from reports by two employees. Which worker is more likely to be promoted?

   a. The spring line failed by 20 percent in the meeting of projected profit expectations. Which were issued in January of this year.

   b. Profits from our spring line were disappointing. They fell 20 percent short of January's predictions.

9. The following paragraphs are taken from two job application letters. Which applicant would you favor?

   a. Let me say in closing that their are an array of personal qualities I have presented in this letter, together, these make me hopeful of being interviewed for this attraktive position.

      sincerely yours'
      Brian Davis

   b. I feel I have the qualifications needed to do an excellent job as assistant manager of the jewelry department at Horton's. I look forward to discussing the position further at a personal interview.

      Sincerely yours,
      Richard O'Keeney

In each case, the first choice (*a*) contains sentence-skills mistakes. These mistakes include missing or misplaced commas and misspellings. As a result of such mistakes, clear communication cannot occur—and misunderstandings, lower grades, and missed job opportunities are probable results. The point, then, is that all the rules that make up standard written English should be a priority if you want your writing to be clear and effective.

Success in College

Standard English is essential if you want to succeed in college. Any report, paper, review, essay exam, or assignment you are responsible for should be written in the best standard English you can produce. If you don't do this, it won't matter how fine your ideas are or how hard you worked—most likely, you will receive a lower grade than you would otherwise deserve. In addition, because standard English requires you to express your thoughts in precise, clear sentences, training yourself to follow the rules can help you think more logically. The basic logic you learn to practice at the sentence level will help as you work to produce well-reasoned papers in all your subjects.

Success at Work

Knowing standard English will also help you achieve success on the job. Studies have found repeatedly that skillful communication, more than any other factor, is the key to job satisfaction and steady progress in a career. A solid understanding of standard English is a basic part of this vital ability to communicate. Moreover, most experts agree that we are now living in an "age of information"—a time when people who use language skillfully have a great advantage over those who do not. Fewer of us will be working in factories or at other types of manual labor. Many more of us will be working with information in various forms—accumulating it, processing it, analyzing it. No matter what kind of job you are preparing yourself for, technical or not, you will need to know standard English to keep pace with this new age. Otherwise, you are likely to be left behind, limited to low-paying jobs that offer few challenges or financial rewards.

"Oh, good heavens. We already know EVERYTHING about you. The resume is just to see if you can write a complete sentence." The above cartoon takes a humorous look at the importance of a clearly written resume. What does a poorly written resume say about a job applicant? Why is it important to have a clearly written, understandable resume? On a separate sheet of paper, list five ways a clearly written resume can help you in a job interview.

Success in Everyday Life

Standard English will help you succeed not just at school and work but in everyday life as well. It will help you feel more comfortable, for example, in writing letters to friends and relatives. It will enable you to write effective notes to your children's schools. It will help you get action when you write a letter of complaint to a company about a product. It will allow you to write letters inquiring about bills—hospital, medical, utility, or legal—or about any kind of service. To put it simply, in our daily lives, those who can use and write standard English have more power than those who cannot.

www.mhhe.com/langan

Your Attitude about Writing

Your attitude toward writing is an important part of learning to write well. To get a sense of just how you feel about writing, read the following statements. Put a check beside those statements with which you agree. (This activity is not a test, so try to be as honest as possible.)

_____ 1. A good writer should be able to sit down and write a paper straight through without stopping.

_____ ✓   2. Writing is a skill that anyone can learn with practice.

_____   3. I'll never be good at writing, because I make too many mistakes in spelling, grammar, and punctuation.

_____   4. Because I dislike writing, I always start a paper at the last possible minute.

_____   5. I've always done poorly in English, and I don't expect that to change.

Now read the following comments about these five statements. The comments will help you see if your attitude is hurting or helping your efforts to become a better writer.

1. **A good writer should be able to sit down and write a paper straight through without stopping.**

   The statement is *false*. Writing is, in fact, a process. It is done not in one easy step but in a series of steps, and seldom at one sitting. If you cannot do a paper all at once, you are like most of the other people on the planet. It is harmful to carry around the false idea that writing should be easy.

2. **Writing is a skill that anyone can learn with practice.**

   This statement is *absolutely true*. Writing is a skill, like driving or cooking, that you can master with hard work. If you want to learn to write, you can. It is as simple as that. If you believe this, you are ready to learn how to become a competent writer.

   Some people hold the false belief that writing is a natural gift, which some have and others do not. Because of this belief, they never make a truly honest effort to learn to write—and so they never learn.

3. **I'll never be good at writing, because I make too many mistakes in spelling, grammar, and punctuation.**

   The first concern in good writing should be *content*—what you have to say. Your ideas and feelings are what matter most. You should not worry about spelling, grammar, and punctuation while working on content.

   Unfortunately, some people are so self-conscious about making mistakes that they do not focus on what they want to say. They need to realize that a paper is best done in stages and that the rules can and should wait until a later stage in the writing process. Through review and practice, you will eventually learn how to follow the rules with confidence.

4. **Because I dislike writing, I always start a paper at the last minute.**

   This practice is all too common. You feel you are *going to* do poorly, and then your behavior ensures that you *will* do poorly! Your attitude is so negative that you defeat yourself—not even allowing enough time to really try.

   Again, what you need to realize is that writing is a process. Because it is done in steps, you don't have to get it right all at once. Just get started well in advance. If you allow yourself enough time, you'll find a way to make a paper come together.

5. **I've done poorly in English in the past, and I don't expect that to change now.**

    How you may have performed in the *past* does not control how you can perform in the *present*. Even if you did poorly in English in high school, it is in your power to make this one of your best subjects in college. If you believe writing can be learned, and if you work hard at it, you *will* become a better writer.

In brief, your attitude is crucial. If you believe you are a poor writer and always will be, chances are you will not improve. If you realize you can become a better writer, chances are you will improve. Depending on how you allow yourself to think, you can be your own best friend or your own worst enemy.

How This Book Is Organized

- A good way to get a quick sense of any book is to turn to the table of contents. By referring to the Contents pages, you will see that the book is organized into three basic parts. What are they?

    Part One: Effective Writing

    Part Two: Sentence Skills

    Part Three: Reinforcement of the Skills

- In Part One, the final section of Chapter 3 includes assignments in the *writing process*.

- Part Two deals with sentence skills. The first section is "Sentences." How many sections (skills areas) are covered in all? Count them. *five*

- Part Three reinforces the skills presented in Part Two. What are the three kinds of reinforcement activities in Part Three?

    Combined Mastery Tests

    Editing and Proofreading Tests

    Combined Editing Tests

- Finally, the six appendixes at the end of the book are: *(A) How a Computer Can Help, (B) Parts of Speech, (C) ESL Pointers, (D) Sentence-Skills Diagnostic Test, (E) Sentence-Skills Achievement Test, (F) Answers to Introductory Activities and Practice Exercises in Part Two.*

How to Use This Book

Here is a way to use *Sentence Skills*. First, read and work through Part One, Effective Writing—a guide to the goals of effective writing followed by a series of activities to help you practice and master these goals. Your instructor may direct you to certain activities, depending on your needs.

Second, take the diagnostic test on pages 546–551. By analyzing which sections of the test give you trouble, you will discover which skills you need to concentrate on. When you turn to an individual skill in Part Two, begin by reading and thinking about the introductory activity. Often you will be pleasantly surprised to find that you know more about this area of English than you thought you did. After all, you have probably been speaking English with fluency and ease for many years; you have an instinctive knowledge of how the language works. This knowledge gives you a solid base for refining your skills.

Your third step is to work on the skills in Part Two by reading the explanations and completing the practices. You can check your answers to each practice activity in this part by turning to the answer key at the back of the book (Appendix F). For any answers you got wrong, try to figure out *why* you got them wrong—you want to uncover any weak spots in your understanding.

Your next step is to use the review tests and mastery tests at the end of each chapter in Part Two to evaluate your understanding of a skill in its entirety. Your instructor may also ask you to take the other reinforcement tests in Part Three of the book. To help ensure that you take the time needed to learn each skill thoroughly, the answers to these tests are *not* in the answer key.

The emphasis in this book is on writing clear, error-free sentences. And the heart of the book is the practice material that helps reinforce the sentence skills you learn. A great deal of effort has been taken to make the practices lively and engaging and to avoid the dull, repetitive skills work that has given grammar books such a bad reputation. This text will help you stay interested as you work on the rules of English that you need to learn. The rest is a matter of your personal determination and hard work. If you decide—and only you can decide—that effective writing is important to your school and career goals and that you want to learn the basic skills needed to write clearly and effectively, this book will help you reach those goals.

A Brief Guide to Effective Writing

2

This chapter and Chapter 3 will show you how to write effective paragraphs. The following questions will be answered in turn:

1. What is a paragraph?

2. What are the goals of effective writing?

3. How do you reach the goals of effective writing?

What Is a Paragraph?

A *paragraph* is a series of sentences about one main idea, or *point*. A paragraph typically starts with a point, and the rest of the paragraph provides specific details to support and develop that point.

Consider the following paragraph, written by a student named Gary Callahan.

www.mhhe.com/langan

Returning to School

Starting college at age twenty-nine was difficult. For one thing, I did not have much support from my parents and friends. My father asked, "Didn't you get dumped on enough in high school? Why go back for more?" My mother worried about where the money would come from. My friends seemed threatened. "Hey, there's the college man," they would say when they saw me. Another reason that starting college was hard was that I had bad memories of school. I had spent years of my life sitting in classrooms

---

continued

> completely bored, watching clocks tick ever so slowly toward the final bell. When I was not bored, I was afraid of being embarrassed. Once a teacher called on me and then said, "Ah, forget it, Callahan," when he realized I did not know the answer. Finally, I soon learned that college would give me little time with my family. After work every day, I have just an hour and ten minutes to eat and spend time with my wife and daughter before going off to class. When I get back, my daughter is in bed, and my wife and I have only a little time together. Then the weekends go by quickly, with all the homework I have to do. But I am going to persist because I believe a better life awaits me with a college degree.

The preceding paragraph, like many effective paragraphs, starts by stating a main idea, or point. A *point* is a general idea that contains an opinion. In this case, the point is that starting college at age twenty-nine was not easy.

In our everyday lives, we constantly make points about all kinds of matters. We express all kinds of opinions: "It's fun to connect with old friends on Facebook." "That was a terrible movie." "My psychology instructor is the best teacher I have ever had." "Eating at that restaurant was a mistake." "That team should win the playoff game." "Waitressing is the worst job I ever had." "Our state should allow the death penalty." "Cigarette smoking should be banned everywhere." "I prefer to read newspapers online instead of picking one up at the 7-11." In *talking* to people, we don't always give the reasons for our opinions. But in *writing,* we *must* provide reasons to support our ideas. Only by supplying solid evidence for any point that we make can we communicate effectively with readers.

An effective paragraph, then, must not only make a point but support it with *specific evidence*—reasons, examples, and other details. Such specifics help prove to readers that the point is reasonable. Even if readers do not agree with the writer, at least they have in front of them the evidence on which the writer has based his or her opinion. Readers are like juries; they want to see the evidence so that they can make their own judgments.

Take a moment now to examine the evidence that Gary has provided to back up his point about starting college at twenty-nine. Complete the following outline of Gary's paragraph by summarizing in a few words his reasons and the details that develop them. The first reason and its supporting details are summarized for you as an example.

POINT: Starting college at age twenty-nine was difficult.

REASON 1: *Little support from parents and friends*

DETAILS THAT DEVELOP REASON 1: *Father asked why I wanted to be dumped on again, mother worried about tuition money, friends seemed threatened*

REASON 2: _____

DETAILS THAT DEVELOP REASON 2: _____

REASON 3: _____

DETAILS THAT DEVELOP REASON 3: _____

_____

_____

As the outline makes clear, Gary provides three reasons to support his point about starting college at twenty-nine: (1) he had little support from his friends or parents, (2) he had bad memories of school, and (3) college left him little time with his family. Gary also provides vivid details to back up each of his three reasons. His reasons and descriptive details enable readers to see why he feels that starting college at twenty-nine was difficult.

To write an effective paragraph, then, aim to do what Gary has done: begin by making a point, and then go on to support that point with specific evidence. Finally, like Gary, end your paper with a sentence that rounds off the paragraph and provides a sense of completion.

Why are you in college? On a separate piece of paper, write a sentence on why you are in college and then list three reasons that support your main point for being in college.

The Goals of Effective Writing

Now that you have considered an effective student paragraph, it is time to look at four goals of effective writing.

Goal 1: Make a Point

It is often best to state your point in the first sentence of your paper, just as Gary does in his paragraph about returning to school. The sentence that expresses the main idea, or point, of a paragraph is called the *topic sentence.* Your paper will be unified if you make sure that all the details support the point in your topic sentence. Activities on pages 15–18 will help you learn how to write a topic sentence.

Goal 2: Support the Point

To support your point, you need to provide specific reasons, examples, and other details that explain and develop it. The more precise and particular your supporting details are, the better your readers can "see," "hear," and "feel" them. Activities on pages 18–33 will help you learn how to be specific in your writing.

Goal 3: Organize the Support

You will find it helpful to learn two common ways of organizing support in a paragraph—*listing order* and *time order.* You should also learn the signal words, known as *transitions,* that increase the effectiveness of each method. Activities on pages 33–40 will give you practice in the use of listing order and time order, as well as transitions, to organize the supporting details of a paragraph.

Goal 4: Write Error-Free Sentences

If you use correct spelling and follow the rules of grammar, punctuation, and usage, your sentences will be clear and well written. But by no means must you have all that information in your head. Even the best of writers need to use reference materials to be sure their writing is correct. So when you write your papers, keep a good dictionary and grammar handbook (you can use Part Two of this book) nearby.

In general, however, save them for after you've gotten your ideas firmly down in writing. You'll see in the next part of this guide that Gary made a number of sentence errors as he worked on his paragraph. But he simply ignored them until he got to a later draft of his paper, when there would be time enough to make the needed corrections.

Activities in the Goals of Effective Writing

The following series of activities will strengthen your understanding of the four goals of effective writing and how to reach those goals. The practice will also help you prepare for the demands of your college classes.

Your instructor may ask you to do the entire series of activities or may select those activities most suited to your particular needs.

www.mhhe.com/langan

Activities in Goal 1: Make a Point

Effective writing advances a point, or main idea, in a general statement known as the *topic sentence*. Other sentences in the paragraph provide specific support for the topic sentence.

The activities in this section will give you practice in the following:

- Identifying the Point
- Understanding the Topic Sentence
- Identifying Topics, Topic Sentences, and Support

Identifying the Point

Each group of sentences below could be written as a short paragraph. Circle the letter of the topic sentence in each case. To find the topic sentence, ask yourself, "Which is a general statement supported by the specific details in the other three statements?"

Begin by trying the example below. First circle the letter of the sentence you think expresses the main idea. Then read the explanation.

Activity

1

EXAMPLE

a. Newspapers are a good source of local, national, and world news.

b. The cartoons and crossword puzzles in newspapers are entertaining.

(c.) Newspapers have a lot to offer.

d. Newspapers often include coupons worth far more than the cost of the paper.

> **EXPLANATION**   Sentence *a* explains one important benefit of newspapers. Sentences *b* and *d* provide other specific advantages of newspapers. In sentence *c,* however, no one specific benefit is explained. Instead, the words "a lot to offer" refer only generally to such benefits. Therefore sentence *c* is the topic sentence; it expresses the main idea. The other sentences support that idea by providing examples.

1. a. Even when Food City is crowded, there are only two cash registers open.
    b. The frozen foods are often partially thawed.
    c. I will never shop at Food City again.
    d. The market doesn't accept Internet coupons.

2. a. Buy only clothes that will match what's already in your closet.
    b. To be sure you're getting the best price, shop in a number of stores before buying.
    c. Avoid trendy clothes; buy basic pieces that never go out of style.
    d. By following a few simple rules, you can have nice clothes without spending a fortune.

3. a. Once my son said a vase jumped off the shelf by itself.
    b. When my son breaks something, he always has an excuse.
    c. He claimed that my three-month-old daughter climbed out of her crib and knocked a glass over.
    d. Another time, he said an earthquake must have caused a mirror to crack.

4. a. Mars should be the first planet explored by astronauts.
    b. Astronauts could mine Mars for aluminum, magnesium, and iron.
    c. The huge volcano on Mars would be fascinating to study.
    d. Since Mars is close to Earth, we might want to have colonies there one day.

5. a. Instead of talking on the telephone, we send text-messages.
    b. People rarely talk to one another these days.
    c. Rather than talking with family members, we sit silently in front of our TV sets all evening.
    d. In cars, we ignore our traveling companions to listen to the radio.

Understanding the Topic Sentence

As already explained, most paragraphs center on a main idea, which is often expressed in a topic sentence. An effective topic sentence does two things. First, it presents the topic of the paragraph. Second, it expresses the writer's attitude or opinion or idea about the topic. For example, look at the following topic sentence:

> *Professional athletes are overpaid.*

In the topic sentence, the topic is *professional athletes;* the writer's idea about the topic is that professional athletes *are overpaid.*

For each topic sentence below, underline the topic and double-underline the point of view that the writer takes toward the topic.

Activity

2

EXAMPLES

Living in a small town has many advantages.

Talking on a cell phone while driving should be banned in every state.

1. The apartments on Walnut Avenue are a fire hazard.

2. Losing my job turned out to have benefits.

3. Blues is the most interesting form of American music.

4. Our neighbor's backyard is a dangerous place.

5. Paula and Jeff are a stingy couple.

6. Snakes do not deserve their bad reputation.

7. Pollution causes many problems in American cities.

8. New fathers should receive "paternity leave."

9. People with low self-esteem often need to criticize others.

10. Learning to write effectively is largely a matter of practice.

Identifying Topics, Topic Sentences, and Support

The following activity will sharpen your sense of the differences between topics, topic sentences, and supporting sentences.

Each group of items below includes one topic, one main idea (expressed in a topic sentence), and two supporting details for that idea. In the space provided, label each item with one of the following:

Activity

3

> *T* — topic
> *MI* — main idea
> *SD* — supporting details

1. __SD__   a. The weather in the summer is often hot and sticky.

   __MI__   b. Summer can be an unpleasant time of year.

   __T__   c. Summer.

   __SD__   d. Bug bites, poison ivy, and allergies are a big part of summertime.

2. __MI__   a. The new Ultimate sports car is bound to be very popular.

   __SD__   b. The company has promised to provide any repairs needed during the first three years at no charge.

   __SD__   c. Because it gets thirty miles per gallon of gas, it offers real savings on fuel costs.

   __T__   d. The new Ultimate sports car.

3. __MI__   a. Decorating an apartment doesn't need to be expensive.

   __SD__   b. A few plants add a touch of color without costing a lot of money.

   __SD__   c. Inexpensive braided rugs can be bought to match nearly any furniture.

   __T__   d. Decorating an apartment.

4. __SD__   a. Long practice sessions and busy game schedules take too much time away from schoolwork.

   __T__   b. High school sports.

   __SD__   c. The competition between schools may become so intense that, depending on the outcome of one game, athletes are either adored or scorned.

   __MI__   d. High school sports put too much pressure on young athletes.

5. __SD__   a. After mapping out the best route to your destination, phone ahead for motel reservations.

   __T__   b. A long car trip.

   __MI__   c. Following a few guidelines before a long car trip can help you avoid potential problems.

   __SD__   d. Have your car's engine tuned as well, and have the tires, brakes, and exhaust system inspected.

Activities in Goal 2: Support the Point

Effective writing gives support—reasons, facts, examples, and other evidence—for each main point. While main points are general (see page 15), support is *specific;* it provides the details that explain the main point.

To write well, you must know the difference between general and specific ideas. It is helpful to realize that you use general and specific ideas all the time in your everyday life. For example, in choosing a DVD to rent, you may think, "Which should I rent, an action movie, a comedy, or a romance?" In such a case, *DVD* is the general idea, and *action movie, comedy,* and *romance* are the specific ideas.

www.mhhe.com/langan

Or you may decide to begin an exercise program. In that case, you might consider walking, jumping rope, or lifting weights. In this case, *exercise* is the general idea, and *walking, jumping rope,* and *lifting weights* are the specific ideas.

Or if you are talking to a friend about a date that didn't work out well, you may say, "The dinner was terrible, the car broke down, and we had little to say to each other." In this case, the general idea is *the date didn't work out well,* and the specific ideas are the three reasons you named.

The activities in this section will give you practice in the following:

- Understanding General and Specific Ideas
- Recognizing Specific Details
- Providing Specific Details
- Selecting Details That Fit
- Providing Details That Fit
- Providing Details in a Paragraph

Understanding General and Specific Ideas

Each group of words consists of one general idea and four specific ideas. The general idea includes all the specific ideas. Underline the general idea in each group.

Activity

4

EXAMPLE

jeep   van   truck   <u>vehicle</u>   sedan

1. salty   bitter   <u>flavor</u>   sweet   sour

2. <u>jewelry</u>   necklace   ring   earrings   bracelet

3. dime   nickel   <u>coin</u>   quarter   half-dollar

4. fax machine   copier   computer   calculator   <u>office machine</u>

5. theft   murder   rape   <u>crime</u>   holdup

6. cracker   <u>snack</u>   carrot stick   cookie   popcorn

7. mascara   <u>cosmetic</u>   foundation   lipstick   eyeshadow

8. yes   no   I don't know   <u>answer</u>   maybe

9. <u>yard work</u>   mowing   planting   trimming hedges   feeding plants

10. job interviews   weddings   car accidents   being fired   <u>stressful times</u>

Activity

5

In each item below, one idea is general and the others are specific. The general idea includes the specific ones. In the spaces provided, write in two more specific ideas that are covered by the general idea.

EXAMPLE

General: exercises
Specific: chin-ups, lunges, _____*sit-ups*_____ , _____*push-ups*_____

1. *General:* pizza toppings
   Specific: sausage, mushrooms, _____Onions_____ , _____Peperoni_____

2. *General:* furniture
   Specific: rocking chair,
   coffee table, _____Couch_____ , _____Rug_____

3. *General:* magazines
   Specific: Reader's Digest,
   Newsweek, _____Sports Illustrated_____ Maximun

4. *General:* birds
   Specific: eagle, pigeon, _____Duck_____ , _____Flamingo_____

5. *General:* types of music
   Specific: jazz, classical, _____Rap_____ , _____Hiphop_____

6. *General:* cold symptoms
   Specific: aching muscles,
   watery eyes, _____Synus infection_____ , _____Cough_____

7. *General:* children's games
   Specific: hopscotch, dodgeball, _____Soccer_____ , _____Kickball._____

8. *General:* transportation
   Specific: plane, motorcycle, _____Car_____ , _____scooter_____

9. *General:* city problems
   Specific: overcrowding,
   pollution, _____Traffic_____ , _____tourist_____

10. *General:* types of TV shows
    Specific: cartoons,
    situation comedies, _____Horror_____ , _____Soap operas_____

Read each group of specific ideas below. Then circle the letter of the general idea that tells what the specific ideas have in common. Note that the general idea should not be too broad or too narrow. Begin by trying the example item, and then read the explanation that follows.

EXAMPLE

Specific ideas: peeling potatoes, washing dishes, cracking eggs, cleaning out refrigerator

The general idea is

a. household jobs.

b. kitchen tasks.

c. steps in making dinner.

EXPLANATION   It is true that the specific ideas are all household jobs, but they have in common something even more specific—they are all tasks done in the kitchen. Therefore answer *a* is too broad, and the correct answer is *b*. Answer *c* is too narrow because it doesn't cover all the specific ideas. While two of them could be steps in making a dinner ("peeling potatoes" and "cracking eggs"), two have nothing to do with making dinner.

---

1. *Specific ideas:* crowded office, rude co-workers, demanding boss, unreasonable deadlines

    The general idea is

    a. problems.

    b. work problems.

    c. problems with work schedules.

2. *Specific ideas:* trout, whales, salmon, frogs

    The general idea is

    a. animals.

    b. fish.

    c. animals living in water.

3. *Specific ideas:* "Go to bed." "Pick up that trash." "Run twenty laps." "Type this letter."

    The general idea is

    a. remarks.

    b. orders.

    c. the boss's orders.

4. *Specific ideas:* "I had no time to study." "The questions were unfair." "I had a headache." "The instructor didn't give us enough time."

The general idea is

a. statements.

b. excuses for being late.

c. excuses for not doing well on a test.

5. *Specific ideas:* driving with expired license plates, driving over the speed limit, parking without putting money in the meter, driving without a license

The general idea is

a. ways to cause a traffic accident.

b. traffic problems.

c. ways to get a ticket.

Activity

7

In the following items, the specific ideas are given but the general ideas are unstated. Fill in the blanks with the unstated general ideas.

EXAMPLE

General idea: ___car problems___

Specific ideas: flat tire   dented bumper
                    cracked windshield   dirty oil filter

1. *General idea:* ___Family___

Specific ideas: nephew   grandmother
                    aunt   cousin

2. *General idea:* ___Outdoors___

Specific ideas: camping   hiking
                    fishing   hunting

3. *General idea:* ___Cleaning untensils___

Specific ideas: broom   sponge
                    mop   glass cleaner

4. *General idea:* ___Dogs___

Specific ideas: fleas in carpeting   loud barking
                    tangled fur   veterinary bills

5. *General idea:* ___Health problems___

Specific ideas: diabetes   cancer
                    appendicitis   broken leg

Recognizing Specific Details

Specific details are examples, reasons, particulars, and facts. Such details are needed to support and explain a topic sentence effectively. They provide the evidence needed for us to understand, as well as to feel and experience, a writer's point.

Below is a topic sentence followed by two sets of supporting sentences. Put a check mark next to the set that provides sharp, specific details.

Topic sentence: Ticket sales for a recent U2 concert proved that the rock band is still very popular.

_____ a. Fans came from everywhere to buy tickets to the concert. People wanted good seats and were willing to endure a great deal of various kinds of discomfort as they waited in line for many hours. Some people actually waited for days, sleeping at night in uncomfortable circumstances. Good tickets were sold out extremely quickly.

✓ _____ b. The first person in the long ticket line spent three days standing in the hot sun and three nights sleeping on the concrete without even a pillow. The man behind her waited equally long in his wheelchair. The ticket window opened at 10:00 A.M, and the tickets for the good seats—those in front of the stage—were sold out an hour later.

EXPLANATION   The second set (*b*) provides specific details. Instead of a vague statement about fans who were "willing to endure a great deal of various kinds of discomforts," we get vivid details we can see and picture clearly: "three days standing in the hot sun," "three nights sleeping on the concrete without even a pillow," "The man behind her waited equally long in his wheelchair."

Instead of a vague statement that tickets were "sold out extremely quickly," we get exact and vivid details: "The ticket window opened at 10:00 A.M., and the tickets for the good seats—those in front of the stage—were sold out an hour later."

Specific details are often like a movie script. They provide us with such clear pictures that we could make a film of them if we wanted to. You would know just how to film the information given in the second set of sentences. You would show the fans in line under a hot sun and, later, sleeping on the concrete. The first person in line would be shown sleeping without a pillow under her head. You would show tickets finally going on sale, and after an hour you could show the ticket seller explaining that all the seats in front of the stage were sold out.

continued

In contrast, the writer of the first set of sentences (*a*) fails to provide the specific information needed. If you were asked to make a film based on set *a*, you would have to figure out on your own just what particulars to show.

When you are working to provide specific supporting information in a paper, it might help to ask yourself, "Could someone easily film this information?" If the answer is yes, your supporting details are specific enough for your readers to visualize.

Activity

8

Each topic sentence below is followed by two sets of supporting details. Write *S* (for *specific*) in the space next to the set that provides specific support for the point. Write *G* (for *general*) next to the set that offers only vague, general support.

> HINT Which set of supporting details could you more readily use in a film?

1. *Topic sentence:* The West Side shopping mall is an unpleasant place.

    _✓___ a. The floors are covered with cigarette butts, dirty paper plates, and spilled food. The stores are so crowded I had to wait twenty minutes just to get a dressing room to try on a shirt.

    _____ b. It's very dirty, and not enough places are provided for trash. The stores are not equipped to handle the large number of shoppers that often show up.

2. *Topic sentence:* Our golden retriever is a wonderful pet for children.

    _____ a. He is gentle, patient, eager to please, and affectionate. Capable of following orders, he is also ready to think for himself and find solutions to a problem. He senses children's moods and goes along with their wishes.

    _✓___ b. He doesn't bite, even when children pull his tail. After learning to catch a ball, he will bring it back again and again, seemingly always ready to play. If the children don't want to play anymore, he will just sit by their side, gazing at them with his faithful eyes.

3. *Topic sentence:* My two-year-old daughter's fearlessness is a constant source of danger to her.

    _____ a. She doesn't realize that certain activities are dangerous. Even when I warn her, she will go ahead and do something that could hurt her. I have to constantly be on the lookout for dangerous situations and try to protect her from them.

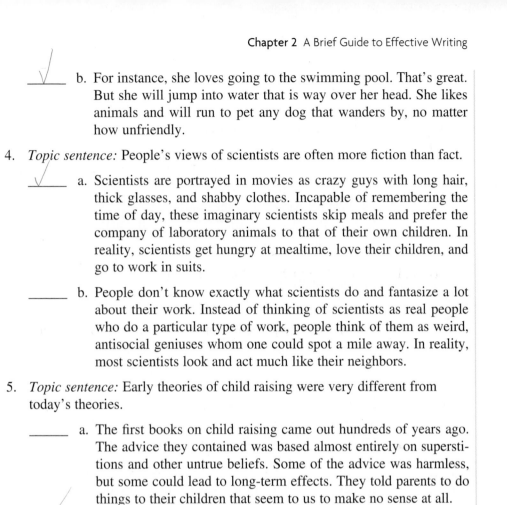

_____ b. For instance, she loves going to the swimming pool. That's great. But she will jump into water that is way over her head. She likes animals and will run to pet any dog that wanders by, no matter how unfriendly.

4. *Topic sentence:* People's views of scientists are often more fiction than fact.

   _____ a. Scientists are portrayed in movies as crazy guys with long hair, thick glasses, and shabby clothes. Incapable of remembering the time of day, these imaginary scientists skip meals and prefer the company of laboratory animals to that of their own children. In reality, scientists get hungry at mealtime, love their children, and go to work in suits.

   _____ b. People don't know exactly what scientists do and fantasize a lot about their work. Instead of thinking of scientists as real people who do a particular type of work, people think of them as weird, antisocial geniuses whom one could spot a mile away. In reality, most scientists look and act much like their neighbors.

5. *Topic sentence:* Early theories of child raising were very different from today's theories.

   _____ a. The first books on child raising came out hundreds of years ago. The advice they contained was based almost entirely on superstitions and other untrue beliefs. Some of the advice was harmless, but some could lead to long-term effects. They told parents to do things to their children that seem to us to make no sense at all.

   _____ b. One early book, for example, advised mothers not to breast-feed their babies right after feeling anger because the anger would go into the milk and injure the child. Another told parents to begin toilet training their children at the age of three weeks and to tie their babies' arms down for several months to prevent thumb sucking.

At several points in each of the following paragraphs, you are given a choice of two sets of supporting details. Write *S* (for *specific*) in the space next to the set that provides specific support for the point. Write *G* (for *general*) next to the set that offers only vague, general support.

Activity

9

Paragraph 1
My daughter is as shy as I am, and it breaks my heart to see her dealing with the same problems I had to deal with in my childhood because of my shyness. I feel very sad for her when I see the problems she has making friends.

_____ a. It takes her a long time to begin to do the things other children do to make friends, and her feelings get hurt very easily over one thing and another. She is not at all comfortable about making connections with her classmates at school.

✓ b. She usually spends Christmas vacation alone because by that time of year she doesn't have friends yet. Only when her birthday comes in the summer is she confident enough to invite school friends to her party. Once she sends out the invitations, she almost sleeps by the telephone, waiting for the children to respond. If they say they can't come, her eyes fill with tears.

I recognize very well her signs of shyness, which make her look smaller and more fragile than she really is.

✓ c. When she has to talk to someone she doesn't know well, she speaks in a whisper and stares sideways. Pressing her hands together, she lifts her shoulders as though she wished she could hide her head between them.

_____ d. When she is forced to talk to anyone other than her family and her closest friends, the sound of her voice and the position of her head change. Even her posture changes in a way that makes it look as if she's trying to make her body disappear.

It is hard for me to watch her passing unnoticed at school.

_____ e. She never gets chosen for a special job or privilege, even though she tries her best, practicing in privacy at home. She just doesn't measure up. Worst of all, even her teacher seems to forget her existence much of the time.

✓ f. Although she rehearses in our basement, she never gets chosen for a good part in a play. Her voice is never loud or clear enough. Worst of all, her teacher doesn't call on her in class for days at a time.

Paragraph 2

It is said that the dog is man's best friend, but I strongly believe that the honor belongs to my computer. A computer won't fetch a stick for me, but it can help me entertain myself in many ways.

_____ a. If I am bored, tired, or out of ideas, the computer allows me to explore things that interest me such as anything relating to the world of professional sports.

_____ ✓ b. The other day, I used my computer to visit the National Football League's Web site. I was then able to get injury updates for players on my favorite team, the Philadelphia Eagles.

While the dog is a faithful friend, it does not allow me to be a more responsible person the way my computer does.

_____ ✓ c. I use my computer to pay all my bills automatically over the Internet. I also use it to balance my checkbook and keep track of my expenses. Now I always know how much money is in my account at the end of the month.

_____ d. The computer helps me be responsible with financial matters because it records my transactions. With the computer I have access to more information, which allows me to make good decisions with my money.

A dog might help me meet strangers I see in the park, but the computer helps me meet people who share my interests.

_____ e. With my computer, I can go online and find people with every type of hobby or interest. Thousands of online chat rooms and discussion groups are available featuring people from all over the country—and the world. The computer can even allow me to develop meaningful personal relationships with others.

_____ ✓ f. Two months ago, I discovered a Web site for people in my community who enjoy hiking. I'm planning to meet a group next Saturday for a day hike. And earlier this year, I met my wonderful fiancée, Shelly, through a computer dating service.

Providing Specific Details

Each of the following sentences contains a general word or words, set off in *italic* type. Substitute sharp, specific words in each case.

Activity 10

EXAMPLE

After the parade, the city street was littered with *garbage*.

After the parade, the city street was littered with multicolored confetti, dirty popcorn, and lifeless balloons.

1. If I had enough money, I'd visit *several places*.

   If I had enough money, I'd visit Paris, Africa, Europe, and Australia.

2. It took her *a long time* to get home.

   It took her a hour to get home
   Traffic, flight delay, Car trouble, weather

3. Ron is often stared at because of his *unusual hair color and hairstyle*.

   Ron is often stared at because of his
   Red Afro ; Design ; Blonde Spikes,

4. After you pass *two buildings,* you'll see my house on the left.

   After you pass glass Sky Scrapers, you'll
   See my house on the left.

5. Nia's purse is crammed with *lots of stuff.*

   Nia's purse is crammed with Makeup;
   Mirror; gum.

6. I bought *some junk food* for the long car trip.

   I bought some chocolate for the long
   car trip.

7. The floor in the front of my car is covered with *things.*

   The floor in the front of my car is covered
   with oil.

8. When his mother said no to his request for a toy, the child *reacted strongly.*

   When his mother said no to his request for
   a toy, the child cried.

9. Devan gave his girlfriend a *surprise present* for Valentine's Day.

   Devan gave his girlfriend a Rose for
   Valentine's Day

10. My cat can *do a wonderful trick.*

    My cat can roll around.

Selecting Details That Fit

The details in your paper must all clearly relate to and support your opening point. If a detail does not support your point, leave it out. Otherwise, your paper will lack unity. For example, see if you can circle the letters of the two sentences that do *not* support the topic sentence below.

> *Topic sentence:* Mario is a very talented person.
> a. Mario is always courteous to his professors.
> b. He has created beautiful paintings in his art course.
> c. Mario is the lead singer in a local band.
> d. He won an award in a photography contest.
> e. He is hoping to become a professional photographer.

> **EXPLANATION**   Being courteous may be a virtue, but it is not a talent, so sentence *a* does not support the topic sentence. Also, Mario's desire to become a professional photographer tells us nothing about his talent; thus sentence *e* does not support the topic sentence either. The other three statements all clearly back up the topic sentence. Each in some way supports the idea that Mario is talented—in art, as a singer, or as a photographer.

In each group below, circle the two items that do *not* support the topic sentence.

Activity

11

1. *Topic sentence:* Carla seems attracted only to men who are unavailable.
   a. She once fell in love with a man serving a life sentence in prison.
   b. Her parents worry about her inability to connect with a nice single man.
   c. She wants to get married and have kids before she is thirty.
   d. Her current boyfriend is married.
   e. Recently she had a huge crush on a movie star.

2. *Topic sentence:* Some dog owners have little consideration for other people.
   a. Obedience lessons can be a good experience for both the dog and the owner.
   b. Some dog owners let their dogs leave droppings on the sidewalk or in other people's yards.
   c. They leave the dog home alone for hours, barking and howling and waking the neighbors.
   d. Some people keep very large dogs in small apartments.
   e. Even when small children are playing nearby, they let their bad-tempered dogs run loose.

3. *Topic sentence:* Dr. Eliot is not a good teacher.
    a. He cancels class frequently with no explanation.
    b. When a student asks a question that he can't answer, he becomes irritated with the student.
    c. He got his Ph.D at a university in another country.
    d. He's taught at the college for many years and is on a number of faculty committees.
    e. He puts off grading papers until the end of the semester and then returns them all at once.

4. *Topic sentence:* Some doctors seem to think it is all right to keep patients waiting.
    a. Pharmaceutical sales representatives sometimes must wait hours to see a doctor.
    b. The doctors stand in the hallway chatting with nurses and secretaries even when they have a waiting room full of patients.
    c. Patients sometimes travel long distances to consult with a particular doctor.
    d. When a patient calls before an appointment to see if the doctor is on time, the answer is often yes even when the doctor is two hours behind schedule.
    e. Some doctors schedule appointments in a way that ensures long lines, to make it appear that they are especially skillful.

5. *Topic sentence:* Several factors were responsible for the staggering loss of lives when the *Titanic* sank.
    a. Over 1,500 people died in the *Titanic* disaster; only 711 survived.
    b. Despite warnings about the presence of icebergs, the captain allowed the *Titanic* to continue at high speed.
    c. If the ship had hit the iceberg head on, its watertight compartments might have kept it from sinking; however, it hit on the side, resulting in a long, jagged gash through which water poured in.
    d. The *Titanic*, equipped with the very best communication systems available in 1912, sent out SOS messages.
    e. When the captain gave orders to abandon the *Titanic*, many passengers refused because they believed the ship was unsinkable, so many lifeboats were only partly filled.

Use *listing order* to arrange the scrambled list of sentences below. Number each supporting sentence 1, 2, 3,... so that you go from the least important item to what is presented as the most important item.

Note that transitions will help by making clear the relationships between some of the sentences.

Activity 16

Topic sentence: I am no longer a big fan of professional sports, for a number of reasons.

_____ Basketball and hockey continue well into the baseball season, and football doesn't have its Super Bowl until the middle of winter, when basketball should be at center stage.

_____ In addition, I detest the high fives, taunting, and trash talk that so many professional athletes now indulge in during games.

_____ Second, I am bothered by the length of professional sports seasons.

_____ Also, professional athletes have no loyalty to a team or city as they greedily sell their abilities to the highest bidder.

_____ For one thing, greed is the engine running professional sports.

_____ There are numerous news stories of professional athletes in trouble with the law because of drugs, guns, fights, traffic accidents, or domestic violence.

_____ After a good year, athletes making millions become unhappy if they aren't rewarded with a new contract calling for even more millions.

_____ But the main reason I've become disenchanted with professional sports is the disgusting behavior of so many of its performers.

Use *time order* to arrange the scrambled sentences below. Number the supporting sentences in the order in which they occur in time (1, 2, 3,...).

Note that transitions will help by making clear the relationships between sentences.

Activity 17

Topic sentence: If you are a smoker, the following steps should help you quit.

_____ Before your "quit day" arrives, have a medical checkup to make sure it will be all right for you to begin an exercise program.

_____ You should then write down on a card your decision to quit and the date of your "quit day."

_____ When your "quit day" arrives, stop smoking and start your exercise program.

_____ Finally, remind yourself repeatedly how good you will feel when you can confidently tell yourself and others that you are a nonsmoker.

_____ Place the card in a location where you will be sure to see it every day.

_____ When you begin this exercise program, be sure to drink plenty of water every day and to follow a sensible diet.

_____ After making a definite decision to stop smoking, select a specific "quit day."

_____ Eventually, your exercise program should include activities strenuous enough to strengthen your lung capacity and your overall stamina.

Activities in Goal 4: Write Error-Free Sentences

www.mhhe.com/langan

Effective writing is free of errors that distract or confuse readers. Whether you are writing a paragraph, letter, job application, or resume, you must learn to write clear, error-free sentences. The activities in Part Two of this book will help you do just that.

The Writing Process

Steps in the Writing Process

Even professional writers do not sit down and write a paper automatically, in one draft. Instead, they have to work on it a step at a time. Writing a paper is a process that can be divided into the following steps:

- *Step 1:* Getting Started through Prewriting
- *Step 2:* Preparing a Scratch Outline
- *Step 3*: Writing the First Draft
- *Step 4:* Revising
- *Step 5:* Editing and Proofreading

These steps are described on the following pages.

Step 1: Getting Started through Prewriting

What you need to learn first are strategies for working on a paper. These strategies will help you do the thinking needed to figure out both the point you want to make and the support you have for that point.

There are several *prewriting strategies*—strategies you use before writing the first draft of your paper:

- Freewriting
- Questioning
- Clustering
- Making a list

Freewriting

Freewriting is just sitting down and writing whatever comes into your mind about a topic. Do this for ten minutes or so. Write without stopping and without worrying at all about spelling, grammar, or the like. Simply get down on paper all the information about the topic that occurs to you.

Here is the freewriting Gary did on his problems with returning to school. Gary had been given the assignment "Write about a problem you are facing at the present time." Gary felt right away that he could write about his college situation. He began prewriting as a way to explore and generate details on his topic.

EXAMPLE OF FREEWRITING

One thing I want to write about is going back to school. At age twenty-nine. A lot to deal with. I sometimes wonder if Im nuts to try to do this or just stupid. I had to deal with my folks when I decided. My dad hated school. He knew when to quit, I'll say that for him. But he doesn't understand Im different. I have a right to my own life. And I want to better myself. He teases me alot. Says things like didnt you get dumped on enough in high school, why go back for more. My mom doesnt understand either. Just keeps worring about where the money was coming from. Then my friends. They make fun of me. Also my wife has to do more of the heavy house stuff because I'm out so much. Getting back to my friends, they say dumb things to get my goat. Like calling me the college man or saying ooh, we'd better watch our grammer. Sometimes I think my dads right, school was no fun for me. Spent years just sitting in class waiting for final bell so I could escape. Teachers didnt help me or take an intrest, some of them made me feel like a real loser. Now things are different and I like most of my teachers. I can talk to the teacher after class or to ask questions if I'm confused. But I really need more time to spend with family, I hardly see them any more. What I am doing is hard all round for them and me.

What electronic devices do you consider essential to your everyday life? What electronic devices could you live without? On a separate piece of paper, freewrite for several minutes on what you would do if you could not use one of your essential electronic devices, such as a cell phone, for a week.

Notice that there are problems with spelling, grammar, and punctuation in Gary's freewriting. Gary is not worried about such matters, nor should he be. He is just concentrating on getting ideas and details down on paper. He knows that it is best to focus on one thing at a time. At this stage, he just wants to write out thoughts as they come to him, to do some thinking on paper.

You should take the same approach when freewriting: explore your topic without worrying at all about being "correct." At this early stage of the writing process, focus all your attention on figuring out what you want to say.

Questioning

Questioning means that you think about your topic by writing down a series of questions and answers about it. Your questions can start with words like *what, when, where, why,* and *how.*

Here are some questions that Gary might have asked while developing his paper, as well as some answers to those questions.

EXAMPLE OF QUESTIONING

Why do I have a problem with returning to school?	My parents and friends don't support me.
How do they not support me?	Dad asks why I want to be dumped on more. Mom is upset because college costs lots of money. Friends tease me about being a college man.
When do they not support me?	When I go to my parents' home for Friday night visits, when my friends see me walking toward them.
Where do I have this problem?	At home, where I barely see my wife and daughter before having to go to class, and where I have to let my wife do house things on weekends while I'm studying.
Why else do I have this problem?	High school was bad experience.
What details back up the idea that high school was bad experience?	Sat in class bored, couldn't wait to get out, teachers didn't help me. One embarrassed me when I didn't know the answer.

Clustering

Clustering is another prewriting strategy that can be used to generate material for a paper. It is helpful for people who like to do their thinking in a visual way.

In *clustering,* you begin by stating your subject in a few words in the center of a blank sheet of paper. Then as ideas come to you, put them in ovals, boxes, or circles around the subject, and draw lines to connect them to the subject. Put minor ideas or details in smaller boxes or circles, and also use connecting lines to show how they relate.

Keep in mind that there is no right or wrong way of clustering. It is a way to think on paper about how various ideas and details relate to one another. Below is an example of clustering that Gary might have done to develop his idea.

EXAMPLE OF CLUSTERING

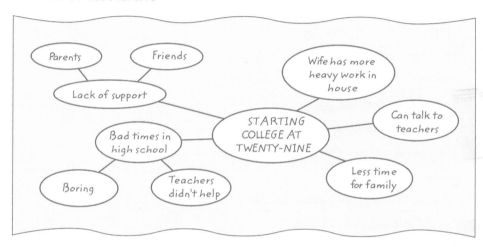

Making a List

In *making a list*—a prewriting strategy also known as *listing, list making,* and *brainstorming*—you make a list of ideas and details that could go into your paper. Simply pile these items up, one after another, without worrying about putting them in any special order. Try to accumulate as many details as you can think of.

After Gary did his freewriting about returning to school, he made up the list of details shown below.

www.mhhe.com/langan

EXAMPLE OF LISTING

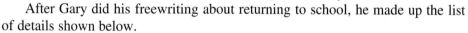

parents give me hard time when they see me

Dad hated school

Dad quit school after eighth grade

Dad says I was dumped on enough in high school

Dad asks why I want to go back for more

Mom also doesnt understand

continued

keeps asking how Ill pay for it

friends give me a hard time too

friends call me college man

say they have to watch their grammar

my wife has more heavy work around the house

also high school had been no fun for me

just sat in class after class

couldnt wait for final bell to ring

wanted to escape

teachers didnt help me

teachers didnt take an interest in me

one called on me, then told me to forget it

I felt like a real loser

I didnt want to go back to his class

now I'm more sure of myself

OK not to know an answer

talk to teachers after class

job plus schoolwork take all my time

get home late, then rush through dinner

then spend evening studying

even have to do homework on weekends

One detail led to another as Gary expanded his list. Slowly but surely, more supporting material emerged that he could use in developing his paper. By the time he had finished his list, he was ready to plan an outline of his paragraph and to write his first draft.

Notice that in making a list, as in freewriting, details are included that will not actually end up in the final paragraph. Gary decided later not to develop the idea that his wife now has more heavy work to do in the house. And he realized that several of his details were about why school is easier in college ("now I'm more sure of myself," "OK not to know an answer," and "talk to instructors after class"); such details were not relevant to his point.

It is natural for a number of such extra or unrelated details to appear as part of the prewriting process. The goal of prewriting is to get a lot of information down on paper. You can then add to, shape, and subtract from your raw material as you take your paper through the series of writing drafts.

Important Points about Prewriting Strategies

Some writers may use only one of the prewriting strategies described here. Others may use bits and pieces of all four strategies. Any one strategy can lead to another. Freewriting may lead to questioning or clustering, which may then lead to a list. Or a writer may start with a list and then use freewriting or questioning to develop items on the list. During this early stage of the writing process, as you do your thinking on paper, anything goes. You should not expect a straight-line progression from the beginning to the end of your paper. Instead, there probably will be a continual moving back and forth as you work to discover your point and decide just how you will develop it.

Keep in mind that prewriting can also help you choose from among several topics. Gary might not have been so sure about which problem to write about. Then he could have made a list of possible topics—areas in his life in which he has had problems. After selecting two or three topics from the list, he could have done some prewriting on each to see which seemed most promising. After finding a likely topic, Gary would have continued with his prewriting activities until he had a solid main point and plenty of support.

Finally, remember that you are not ready to begin writing a paper until you know your main point and many of the details to support it. Don't rush through prewriting. It's better to spend more time on this stage than to waste time writing a paragraph for which you have no solid point and not enough interesting support.

Step 2: Preparing a Scratch Outline

A *scratch outline* is a brief plan for a paragraph. It shows at a glance the point of the paragraph and the main support for that point. It is the logical backbone on which the paper is built.

www.mhhe.com/langan

This rough outline often follows freewriting, questioning, clustering, or listing—or all four. Or it may gradually emerge in the midst of these strategies. In fact, trying to outline is a good way to see if you need to do more prewriting. If a solid outline does not emerge, then you know you need to do more prewriting to clarify your main point or its support. Once you have a workable outline, you may realize, for instance, that you want to do more listing to develop one of the supporting details in the outline.

In Gary's case, as he was working on his list of details, he suddenly discovered what the plan of his paragraph could be. He went back to the list, crossed out items that he now realized did not fit, and added the following comments.

EXAMPLE OF LIST WITH COMMENTS

Starting college at twenty-nine isn't easy—three reasons

parents give me hard time when they see me

Dad hated school

Dad quit school after eighth grade

Dad says I was dumped on enough in high school

Dad asks why I want to go back for more   *Parents and friends*

Mom also doesnt understand   *don't support me*

keeps asking how Ill pay for it

friends give me a hard time too

friends call me college man

say they have to watch their grammar

~~my wife has more heavy work around the house~~

also high school had been no fun for me

just sat in class after class

couldnt wait for final bell to ring

wanted to escape

teachers didnt help me

teachers didnt take an interest in me   *Bad memories*

one called on me, then told me to forget it   *of school*

I felt like a real loser

I didnt want to go back to his class

~~now I'm more sure of myself~~

~~OK not to know an answer~~

~~talk to teachers after class~~

job and schoolwork take all my time

get home late, then rush through dinner   *Not enough time*

then spend evening studying   *with family*

even have to do homework on weekends

Under the list, Gary was now able to prepare his scratch outline.

EXAMPLE OF SCRATCH OUTLINE

> *Starting college at age twenty-nine isn't easy.*
> 1. *Little support from parents or friends*
> 2. *Bad memories of school*
> 3. *Not enough time to spend with family*

After all his preliminary writing, Gary sat back, pleased. He knew he had a promising paper—one with a clear point and solid support. Gary was now ready to write the first draft of his paper, using his outline as a guide.

Step 3: Writing the First Draft

When you write your first draft, be prepared to put in additional thoughts and details that didn't emerge in your prewriting. And don't worry if you hit a snag. Just leave a blank space or add a comment such as "Do later" and press on to finish the paper. Also, don't worry yet about grammar, punctuation, or spelling. You don't want to take time correcting words or sentences that you may decide to remove later. Instead, make it your goal to develop the content of your paper with plenty of specific details.

Here is Gary's first draft.

> ### First Draft
>
> *Last fall, I finaly realized that I was stuck in a dead-end job. I wasnt making enough money and I was bored to tears. I figured I had to get some new skills which meant going back to school. Beginning college at age twenty-nine turned out to be much tougher than I thought it would be. My father didnt understand, he hated school. That's why he quit after eighth grade. He would ask, Didnt you get dumped on enough in high school? Then wondered why I wanted to go back for more of the same thing. My mother was*

continued

> *worried about where the money were coming from and said so. When my friends saw me coming down the st. They would make fun of me with remarks like Hey theres the college man. They may have a point. School never was much fun for me. I spent years just siting in class waiting for the bell to ring. So I could escape. The teachers werent much help to me. One time, a teacher called on me then told me to forget it. I felt like a real loser and didnt want to go back to his class. College takes time away from my family. ADD MORE DETAILS LATER. All this makes it very hard for me.*

After Gary finished the draft, he was able to put it aside until the next day. You will benefit as well if you can allow some time between finishing a draft and starting to revise.

Step 4: Revising

Revising is as much a stage in the writing process as prewriting, outlining, and writing a first draft. *Revising* means rewriting a paper, building on what has been done, to make it stronger. One writer has said about revision, "It's like cleaning house—getting rid of all the junk and putting things in the right order." It is not just "straightening up"; instead, you must be ready to roll up your sleeves and do whatever is needed to create an effective paper. Too many students think that the first draft *is* the paper. They start to become writers when they realize that revising a rough draft three or four times is often at the heart of the writing process.

Here are some quick hints that can help make revision easier:

- Ideally, set your first draft aside for a while. A few hours are fine, but a day or two is best. You can then come back with a fresh, more objective point of view.
- Work from typed or printed text. You'll be able to see the paper more impartially in this way than if you were just looking at your own familiar handwriting.
- Read your draft aloud. Hearing how your writing sounds will help you pick up problems with meaning as well as style.
- As you do all these things, add your thoughts and changes above the lines or in the margins of your paper. Your written comments can serve as a guide when you work on the next draft.

Here is Gary's second draft.

Second Draft

Starting college at age twenty-nine turned out to be really tough. I did not have much support from my parents and friends. My father hated school, so he asked, Didnt you get dumped on enough in high school? Why go back for more? My mother asking about where the money were coming from. Friends would be making fun of me. Hey theres the college man they would say as soon as they saw me. Another factor was what happened to me in high school. I spent years just siting in class waiting for the bell to ring. I was really bored. Also the teachers liked to embaras me. One teacher called on me and then said forget it. He must of relized I didnt know the answer. I felt like a real loser and didnt want to go back in his class for weeks. Finally I've learned that college takes time away from my family. I have to go to work every day. I have a little over one hour to eat dinner and spend time with my wife and daughter. Then I have to go off to class and when I get back my daughter is in bed asleep. My wife and I have only a little time together. On weekends I have lots of homework to do, so the time goes by like a shot. College is hard for me, but I am going to stay there so I can have a better life.

Notice the improvements made in the second draft:

- Gary started by clearly stating the point of his paragraph. He remembered the first goal in effective writing: *Make a point.*

- To keep the focus on his own difficulties, he omitted the detail about his father quitting school. He remembered that the first goal in effective writing is also to *stick to one point,* so the paper will have unity.

- He added more details so that he would have enough support for his reasons why college was hard. He remembered the second goal in effective writing: *Support the point.*

- He inserted transitions to set off the second reason ("Another factor") and third reason ("Finally") why starting college at twenty-nine was difficult for him. He remembered the third goal in effective writing: *Organize the support.*

Gary then went on to revise the second draft. Since he was doing the paper on a computer, he was able to print it out quickly. He double-spaced the lines, allowing room for revisions, which he added in longhand during his third draft. (Note that if you are not using a computer, you may want to do each draft on one side of a page, so that you see your entire paper at one time.) Shown below are some of the changes that Gary made in longhand as he worked on his third draft.

Part of Third Draft

Starting college at age twenty-nine ~~turned out to be really tough.~~ *was difficult.* I did *For one thing* not have much support from my parents and friends. My father ~~hated school, so he~~ asked, Didnt you get dumped on enough in high school? Why go back for more? My mother ~~asking~~ *woried* about where the money were coming from. Friends would ~~be making~~ *make* fun of me. Hey theres the college man they would say as soon as they saw me. Another ~~factor~~ *reason that starting college was hard* was what happened to me in high school. I spent years just siting in class waiting for the ~~bell~~ *final* to ring. I was really bored. Also the teachers liked to embaras me. . . .

After writing these and other changes, Gary typed them into his computer file and printed out the almost-final draft of his paper. He knew he had come to the fourth goal in effective writing: *aim for error-free sentences.*

Step 5: Editing and Proofreading

The next-to-last major stage in the writing process is *editing*—checking a paper for mistakes in grammar, punctuation, usage, and spelling. Students often find it hard to edit a paper carefully. They have put so much work into their writing, or so little, that it's almost painful for them to look at the paper one more time. You may simply have to *will* yourself to carry out this important closing step in the writing process. Remember that eliminating sentence-skills mistakes will improve an average paper and help ensure a strong grade on a good paper. Further, as you get into the habit of checking your papers, you will also get into the habit of using sentence skills consistently. They are an integral part of clear, effective writing. The checklist of sentence skills on the inside back cover of the book will serve as a guide while you are editing your paper.

Here are hints that can help you edit the next-to-final draft of a paper for sentence-skills mistakes.

EDITING HINTS

1. Have at hand two essential tools: a good dictionary (see page 388) and a grammar handbook (you can use Part Two of this book).

2. Use a sheet of paper to cover your essay so that you expose only one sentence at a time. Look for errors in grammar, spelling, and typing. It may help to read each sentence out loud. If the sentence does not read clearly and smoothly, chances are something is wrong.

3. Pay special attention to the kinds of errors you tend to make. For example, if you tend to write run-ons or fragments, be especially on the lookout for these errors.

4. Try to work on a typewritten or word-processed draft, where you'll be able to see your writing more objectively than you can on a handwritten page; use a pen with colored ink so that your corrections will stand out.

Shown below are some of the corrections in spelling, grammar, and punctuation that Gary made when editing his paper.

Part of Gary's Edited Draft

Starting college at age twenty-nine was difficult. For one thing I did not have much support from my parents and friends. My father asked, "Didn't you get dumped on enough in high school? Why go back for more?" My mother ~~woried~~ *worried* about where the money ~~were~~ *was* coming from. Friends would make fun of me. "Hey, there's the college man" they would say as soon as they saw me. . . .

All that remained for Gary to do was to enter in his corrections, print out the final draft of the paper, and proofread it (see the next page for hints on proofreading) for any typos or other careless errors. He was then ready to hand the paper in to his instructor.

Proofreading, the final stage in the writing process, means checking a paper carefully for errors in spelling, grammar, punctuation, and so on. You are ready for this stage when you are satisfied with your choice of supporting details, the order in which they are presented, and the way they and your topic sentence are worded. You will already have attempted to correct all grammar, spelling, and punctuation errors.

At this point in his work, Gary used his dictionary to do final checks on his spelling. He used a grammar handbook (such as the one in Part Two of this text) to be sure about grammar, punctuation, and usage. Gary also read through his paper carefully, looking for typing errors, omitted words, and any other errors he may have missed before. Proofreading is often hard to do—again, students have spent so much time with their work, or so little, that they want to avoid it. But if it is done carefully, this important final step will ensure that your paper looks as good as possible.

PROOFREADING HINTS

1. One helpful trick at this stage is to read your paper out loud. You will probably hear awkward wordings and become aware of spots where the punctuation needs to be improved. Make the changes needed for your sentences to read smoothly and clearly.

2. Another helpful technique is to take a sheet of paper and cover your paragraph so that you expose just one line at a time and check it carefully.

3. A third strategy is to read your paper backward, from the last sentence to the first. This helps keep you from getting caught up in the flow of the paper and missing small mistakes—which is easy to do, since you're so familiar with what you mean to say.

Activities in the Writing Process

These activities will give you practice in some of the prewriting strategies you can use to generate material for a paper. Try to do two or more of these prewriting activities.

Activity

1

Freewriting

On a sheet of paper, freewrite for several minutes about the best or most disappointing friend you ever had. Don't worry about grammar, punctuation, or spelling. Try to write, without stopping, about whatever comes into your head concerning your best or most disappointing friend.

Questioning

Activity

2

On another sheet of paper, answer the following questions about the friend you've started to write about.

1. When did this friendship take place?
2. Where did it take place?
3. What is one reason you liked or were disappointed in this friend? Give one quality, action, comment, etc. Also, give some details to illustrate this quality.
4. What is another reason that you liked or were disappointed in your friend? What are some details that support the second reason?
5. Can you think of a third thing about your friend that you liked or were disappointed in? What are some details that support the third reason?

Clustering

Activity

3

In the center of a blank sheet of paper, write and circle the words *best friend* or *most disappointing friend*. Then, around the circle, add reasons and details about the friend. Use a series of boxes, circles, or other shapes, along with connecting lines, to set off the reasons and details. In other words, try to think about and explore your topic in a very visual way.

Making a List

Activity

4

On separate paper, make a list of details about the friend. Don't worry about putting them in a certain order. Just get down as many details about the friend as occur to you. The list can include specific reasons you liked or were disappointed in the person and specific details supporting those reasons.

Scratch Outline

Activity

5

On the basis of your prewriting, prepare a scratch outline made up of your main idea and the three main reasons you liked or were disappointed in your friend. Use the form below:

_____ was my best *or* most disappointing friend.

*Reason 1:*_____

*Reason 2:*_____

*Reason 3:*_____

Activity 6

First Draft

Now write a first draft of your paper. Begin with your topic sentence, stating that a certain friend was the best or most disappointing one you ever had. Then state the first reason to support your main idea, followed by specific details supporting that reason. Next, state the second reason, again, followed by specific details supporting that reason. Finally, state the third reason, followed by support.

Don't worry about grammar, punctuation, or spelling. Just concentrate on getting down on paper the details about your friend.

Activity 7

Revising the Draft

Ideally, you will have a chance to put your paper aside for a while before writing the second draft. In your second draft, try to do all of the following:

1. Add transition words such as *first of all, another,* and *finally* to introduce each of the three reasons you liked or were disappointed in the friend you're writing about.

2. Omit any details that do not truly support your topic sentence.

3. Add more details as needed, making sure you have plenty of support for each of your three reasons.

4. Check to see that your details are vivid and specific. Can you make a supporting detail more concrete? Are there any persuasive, colorful specifics you can add?

5. Try to eliminate wordiness (see page 443) and clichés (see page 440).

6. In general, improve the flow of your writing.

7. Be sure to include a final sentence that rounds off the paper, bringing it to a close.

Activity 8

Editing and Proofreading

When you have your almost-final draft of the paper, proofread it as follows:

1. Using your dictionary, check any words that you think might be misspelled. Or use a spell-check program on your computer.

2. Using Part Two of this book, check your paper for mistakes in grammar, punctuation, and usage.

3. Read the paper aloud, listening for awkward or unclear spots. Make the changes needed for the paragraph to read smoothly and clearly. Even better, see if you can get another person to read the draft aloud to you. The spots that this person has trouble reading are spots where you may have to do some rewriting.

4. Take a sheet of paper and cover your writing so that you expose and carefully check one line at a time. Or read your writing backward, from the end of the paragraph to the beginning. Look for typing errors, omitted words, and other remaining errors.

Don't fail to edit and proofread carefully. You may be tired of working on your paper at this point, but you want to give the extra effort needed to make it as good as possible. A final push can mean the difference between a higher and a lower grade.

Ten Writing Assignments

Your instructor may ask you to do one or more of the following paragraph writing assignments. Be sure to check the rules for paper format on page 285.

Writing Assignment

A Vivid Memory of Your Mother or Father   1

Think of a particularly clear memory you have of your mother or father. It might be a happy memory that warms your heart. Or it could be humorous, frightening, or enraging. The important thing is that it is a sharp, specific recollection that produces a strong emotional response in you. Then write a paragraph about your memory.

Your goal will be to let the reader see exactly what happened and understand what you felt. To accomplish this, you must provide very specific details. Remember that your reader will have no prior knowledge of your mother or father. You are responsible for painting a "word picture" that will let your reader see your parent the way you saw him or her.

Before you begin writing the paragraph itself, do some prewriting. You might jot down answers to the kind of questions a curious reader would have about your memory. Here are a few such questions: Where did this event take place? When? Who was present? How old was your parent when this occurred? How old were you? What did your parent look like? What did he or she say? How did he or she say it? Why is this memory so vivid for you? The answers to questions like these will provide the kind of concrete detail that will make your paragraph come alive. Begin your paragraph with a summary statement, such as these:

> One of my family's most amusing experiences took place when I found my father sleepwalking in the kitchen.

> Seeing my mother trip on the sidewalk was the beginning of a difficult morning for me.

Your paragraph will probably be organized in time order, describing the events that occurred from beginning to end. You can help your reader understand the sequence of events if you use time transitions such as *first, next, then, later,* and *finally.*

If you prefer, write instead about a memory of another relative.

Writing Assignment

2   A Disagreeable Characteristic

Even the most saintly person has one or more unpleasant traits. Write a paragraph about a particularly disagreeable characteristic of someone you know. Your topic sentence will be a general statement about that person and the quality you've chosen to write about. For example, if you decide to write about your own extreme impatience, your topic sentence might be the following.

> When I let my impatience get out of hand, I often damage my relationships with others.

A paragraph with this topic sentence might list two or three experiences supporting that main idea. Here are two other examples of topic sentences for this paper:

> Our neighbor Mr. Nagle is a cruel person.

> While my minister is basically a kind man, he much prefers hearing his own voice to anyone else's.

Writing Assignment

3   A Life-Changing Event

Write a paragraph about an event in your life that changed the way you think, act, or feel about something or someone. Perhaps you or a family member faced a life-threatening illness, or you recently got married or had a child. You may have been changed by a book or newspaper article you read or a television program you saw. In writing about a life-changing event, consider these topic sentences:

> My life changed forever when my daughter was born.

> Learning how to say no to friends and family has made me a stronger person.

> Seeing my father's heroic battle with lung cancer changed the way I think of him.

> I have had good and bad experiences as a result of losing a hundred pounds.

In Praise of Something   4

We all are fans of something that we feel greatly enriches our life, such as a pet, basketball, or chocolate. Write a paragraph in which your supporting details show the benefits or virtues of something you adore. For instance, you could write about the advantages of having a dog around the house. Use whatever prewriting strategy you choose to help you come up with more benefits or virtues than you need. Then choose two or three you feel you can explain in colorful detail.

One benefit you might list, for instance, is that a dog makes one feel loved. You could illustrate this benefit by describing an experience such as the following:

> A week ago, I spilled hot coffee on a customer's lap. He was not amused. After the customer left—without leaving a tip, of course—the manager walked past me and said quietly, "Strike one!" When I got home that day and collapsed on a chair, my friend Goldie, a cocker spaniel, hopped onto my lap and licked my face with his broad, warm tongue. I could feel the knot in my stomach loosening.

Here's a sample scratch outline for this assignment.

Topic sentence: Having a dog around the house is one of life's rich pleasures.

(1) A dog is entertaining.

(2) A dog brings out the best in a person.

(3) A dog makes a person feel loved.

A Popular Saying   5

It seems there are sayings to cover every type of experience, from our sleeping habits ("Early to bed, early to rise, makes a man healthy, wealthy, and wise") to our expectations ("Hope for the best but expect the worst"). Write a paragraph in which you demonstrate through an experience you have had that a particular saying is either true or false.

Begin your paragraph with a clear statement supporting or opposing the saying, such as "When I painted my house last summer, I learned the truth of the saying 'Haste makes waste'" or "When it comes to escaping a fire, the saying 'Haste makes waste' doesn't apply." Then go on to describe your experience in vivid detail. To help your reader follow the sequence of events involved, use a few time transitions (*before, then, during, now,* and so on). Below are some other popular sayings you might wish to consider using in your paper—or use some other popular saying.

Here today, gone tomorrow.

If you don't help yourself, nobody will.

A penny saved is a penny earned.

The early bird catches the worm.

Curiosity killed the cat.

You get what you pay for.

A rolling stone gathers no moss.

Don't count your chickens before they're hatched.

An ounce of prevention is worth a pound of cure.

A journey of a thousand miles must begin with a single step.

Whatever can go wrong will go wrong.

Don't judge someone until you've walked a mile in his shoes.

Writing Assignment

6 | Writing on the Job

Imagine that at the place where you work, one employee has just quit, creating a new job opening. Since you have been working there for a while, your boss has asked you to write a description of the position. That description, a detailed definition of the job, will be sent to employment agencies. These agencies will be responsible for interviewing candidates. Choose any position you know about, and write a paragraph defining it. First state the purpose of the job, and then list its duties and responsibilities. Finally, describe the qualifications for the position. Below is a sample topic sentence for this assignment.

Purchasing-department secretary is a position in which someone provides a variety of services to the purchasing-department managers.

In a paragraph with the topic sentence above, the writer would go on to list and explain the various services the secretary must provide.

Second Chances

7

Many people have received second chances in life. The news is full of stories in which people have received second chances—in a recent story, for example, a man in Belgium was thought to be brain dead as a result of injuries he suffered in a car crash twenty-three years ago; however, this man was actually conscious the whole time and aware of his surroundings although he could not speak. Through the use of a special electronic keyboard attached to his wheelchair, this man can now communicate with friends and family. Perhaps your second chance is not quite as dramatic as the one presented here. All the same, life is full of second chances.

Think about your life thus far. Have you overcome something that has allowed you a second chance at life? Have you received a second chance in a relationship that you thought was doomed? Did you get a second chance at a job? Freewrite for ten minutes or so about your second chance and what happened in your life to give you that second chance. Then, write a paragraph that begins with a topic sentence something like this: "I received a second chance at my job when I told my supervisor that I would report to work on time every day."

An Embarrassing Moment

8

In a paragraph, tell about a time you felt ashamed or embarrassed. Provide details that show clearly what happened. Explain what you and the other people involved said and did. Also explain how you felt and why you were so uncomfortable.

For example, you might begin with a sentence like this:

I was deeply ashamed when I was caught cheating on a spelling test in fifth grade.

The paragraph could continue by telling how the writer cheated and how he was caught; how the teacher and other students looked, spoke, and acted; what the writer did when he was caught; and what emotions and thoughts the writer experienced throughout the incident.

Below are some other topic sentence possibilities. Develop one of them or a variation on one of them. Feel free as well to come up with and write about an entirely different idea.

- My first real date was the occasion of an embarrassing moment in my life.
- To this day, I wince when I think of an incident that happened to me at a family party.
- An event that occurred in high school makes my cheeks glow hot and red even today.

Writing Assignment

9 A Personal Treasure

Imagine that your apartment or house is burning down. After making sure all the people in your building are safe, you realize you have time to rescue *just one* of your possessions. What would it be? In a paragraph, discuss the item and why it has such importance to you. Be sure you provide supporting details that explain why you value this object. Here are some possible topic sentences for this paragraph:

- If I could save just one of my possessions, it would be my journal.
- My grandmother's wedding ring is the most important object I own.
- Nothing is more valuable to me than my giant photo album.

Writing Assignment

10 Reaching a Goal

Write a paragraph telling of something you wanted very badly but were afraid you would not be able to attain. Describe the struggles you had to overcome to get to your goal. How did you finally reach it? Include some details that communicate how strongly you wanted the goal and how difficult it was to reach. In thinking about a topic for this paper, you may wish to consider the following common goals:

a certain job

enough money for college

a passing grade

quitting smoking or drugs

overcoming an illness

Once you have decided on the goal you wish to write about, write a topic sentence about it such as any of the following:

- After several false starts, I finally quite smoking.
- After gradually changing my attitude about school, I have begun to get good grades.
- Following a careful budget, I was finally able to afford to . . .

PART 2

Sentence Skills

Introduction

Part Two explains the basic skills needed to write clear, error-free sentences. While the skills are presented within five traditional categories (sentences; verbs, pronouns, and agreement; modifiers and parallelism; punctuation and mechanics; word use), each section is self-contained so that you can go directly to the skills you need to work on. Note, however, that you may find it helpful to cover Chapter 4, "Subjects and Verbs," before turning to other skills. Typically, the main features of a skill are presented on the first pages of a section; secondary points are developed later. Numerous activities are provided so that you can practice skills enough to make them habits. The activities are varied and range from underlining answers to writing complete sentences involving the skill in question. One or more review tests at the end of each section offer additional practice activities. Mastery tests conclude each chapter, allowing you to immediately test your understanding of each skill.

What are your plans for the future after you have graduated from college? What five things would you like to do as a result of graduating from college? On a separate piece of paper, using any of the prewriting techniques discussed so far (freewriting, questioning, clustering, making a list), spend time prewriting for a paper on your plans for the future after college.

4

Subjects and Verbs

Introductory Activity

Understanding subjects and verbs is a big step toward mastering many sentence skills. As a speaker of English, you already have an instinctive feel for these **basic building blocks of English sentences.** See if you can insert an appropriate word in each space below. The answer will be a subject.

1. The _Summer_ will soon be over.

2. _Paul_ cannot be trusted.

3. A strange _animal_ appeared in my backyard.

4. _Baseball_ is one of my favorite activities.

Now insert an appropriate word in the following spaces. Each answer will be a verb.

5. The prisoner _yelled_ at the judge.

6. My sister _laughs_ much harder than I do.

7. The players _chanted_ in the locker room.

8. Rob and Marilyn _argued_ with the teacher.

Finally, insert appropriate words in the following spaces. Each answer will be a subject in the first space and a verb in the second.

9. The ___Cat___ almost ___fell___ out of the tree.

10. Many ___people___ today _____ sex and violence.

11. The ___Doctor___ carefully ___examined___ the patient.

12. A ___player___ quickly ___Stole___ the ball.

The basic building blocks of English sentences are subjects and verbs. Understanding them is an important first step toward mastering a number of sentence skills.

Every sentence has a subject and a verb. Who or what the sentence speaks about is called the *subject;* what the sentence says about the subject is called the *verb.* In the following sentences, the subject is underlined once and the verb twice:

1. People gossip.

2. The truck belched fumes.

3. He waved at me.

4. Alaska contains the largest wilderness area in the United States.

5. That woman is a millionaire.

6. The pants feel itchy.

A Simple Way to Find a Subject

To find a subject, ask *who* or *what* the sentence is about. As shown below, your answer is the subject.

Who is the first sentence about? People

What is the second sentence about? The truck

Who is the third sentence about? He

What is the fourth sentence about? Alaska

Who is the fifth sentence about? That woman

What is the sixth sentence about? The pants

It helps to remember that the subject of a sentence is always a *noun* (any person, place, or thing) or a pronoun. A *pronoun* is simply a word like *he, she, it, you,* or *they* used in place of a noun. In the preceding sentences, the subjects are persons (*People, He, woman*), a place (*Alaska*), and things (*truck, pants*). And note that one pronoun (*He*) is used as a subject.

A Simple Way to Find a Verb

To find a verb, ask what the sentence *says* about the subject. As shown below, your answer is the verb.

What does the first sentence *say about* people? They gossip.

What does the second sentence *say about* the truck? It belched (fumes).

What does the third sentence *say about* him? He waved (at me).

What does the fourth sentence *say about* Alaska? It contains (the largest wilderness area in the United States).

What does the fifth sentence *say about* that woman? She is (a millionaire).

What does the sixth sentence *say about* the pants? They feel (itchy).

A second way to find the verb is to put *I, you, he, she, it,* or *they* in front of the word you think is a verb. If the result makes sense, you have a verb. For example, you could put *they* in front of *gossip* in the first sentence above, with the result, *they gossip,* making sense. Therefore, you know that *gossip* is a verb. You could use the same test with the other verbs as well.

Finally, it helps to remember that most verbs show action. In "People gossip," the action is gossiping. In "The truck belched fumes," the action is belching. In "He waved at me," the action is waving. In "Alaska contains the largest wilderness area in the United States," the action is containing.

Certain other verbs, known as *linking verbs,* do not show action. They do, however, give information about the subject of the sentence. In "That woman is a millionaire," the linking verb *is* tells us that the woman is a millionaire. In "The pants feel itchy," the linking verb *feel* gives us the information that the pants are itchy.

Practice

1

In each of the following sentences, draw one line under the subject and two lines under the verb.

To find the subject, ask *who* or *what* the sentence is about. Then, to find the verb, ask what the sentence *says about* the subject.

1. I ate an entire pizza by myself.

2. Alligators swim in that lake.

3. April failed the test.

4. The television movie ended suddenly.

5. Keiko borrowed change for the pay telephone.

6. The children stared in wide-eyed wonderment at the Thanksgiving Day floats.

7. An old newspaper tumbled down the dirty street.

8. Lola starts every morning with a series of yoga exercises.

9. My part-time job limits my study time.

10. The windstorm blew over the storage shed in the backyard.

Follow the directions given for Practice 1. Note that all of the verbs here are linking verbs.

1. My sister is a terrible speller.

2. Potato chips are Ramon's favorite snack.

3. The defendant appeared very nervous on the witness stand.

4. Art became a father at the age of twenty.

5. The ride going somewhere always seems longer than the ride coming back.

6. That apartment building was an abandoned factory two years ago.

7. My first two weeks on the sales job were the worst of my life.

8. The plastic banana split and Styrofoam birthday cake in the bakery window look like real desserts.

9. Jane always feels energized after a cup of coffee.

10. Rooms with white walls seem larger than those with dark-colored walls.

Follow the directions given for Practice 1.

1. That clock runs about five minutes fast.

2. The new player on the team is much too sure of himself.

3. Late-afternoon shoppers filled the aisles of the supermarket.

4. Garbage trucks rumbled down my street on their way to the dump.

5. The children drew pictures on the steamed window.

6. The picture fell suddenly to the floor.

7. Chipmunks live in the woodpile behind my house.

Practice 2

Practice 3

8. Our loud uncle monopolized the conversation at the dinner table.

9. The tomatoes were soft to the touch.

10. The insurance company canceled my policy because of a speeding ticket.

www.mhhe.com/langan

More about Subjects and Verbs

Distinguishing Subjects from Prepositional Phrases

The subject of a sentence never appears within a prepositional phrase. A *prepositional phrase* is simply a group of words beginning with a preposition and ending with the answer to the question *what, when,* or *where.* Here is a list of common prepositions.

Common Prepositions

about	before	by	inside	over
above	behind	during	into	through
across	below	except	of	to
among	beneath	for	off	toward
around	beside	from	on	under
at	between	in	onto	with

When you are looking for the subject of a sentence, it is helpful to cross out prepositional phrases.

~~In the middle of the night,~~ we heard footsteps ~~on the roof.~~

The magazines ~~on the table~~ belong ~~in the garage.~~

~~Before the opening kickoff,~~ a brass band marched ~~onto the field.~~

The hardware store ~~across the street~~ went ~~out of business.~~

~~In spite of our advice,~~ Sally quit her job ~~at Burger King.~~

Practice

4

Cross out prepositional phrases. Then draw a single line under subjects and a double line under verbs.

1. ~~For that course,~~ you need three different books.

2. The key ~~to the front door~~ slipped from ~~my hand into a puddle.~~

3. The checkout lines ~~at the supermarket~~ moved very slowly.

4. With his son, Jamal walked to the playground.

5. No quarrel between good friends lasts for a very long time.

6. In one weekend, Martha planted a large vegetable garden in her backyard.

7. Either of my brothers is a reliable worker.

8. The drawer of the bureau sticks on rainy days.

9. During the movie, several people walked out in protest.

10. At a single sitting, my brother reads five or more comic books.

Verbs of More Than One Word

Many verbs consist of more than one word. Here, for example, are some of the many forms of the verb *help:*

Some Forms of the Verb *Help*

helps	should have been helping	will have helped
helping	can help	would have been helped
is helping	would have been helping	has been helped
was helping	will be helping	had been helped
may help	had been helping	must have helped
should help	helped	having helped
will help	have helped	should have been helped
does help	has helped	had helped

Below are sentences that contain verbs of more than one word:

Yolanda is working overtime this week.

Another book has been written about the Kennedy family.

We should have stopped for gas at the last station.

The game has just been canceled.

TIPS

1. Words like *not, just, never, only,* and *always* are not part of the verb, although they may appear within the verb.

   Yolanda is not working overtime next week.

   The boys should just not have stayed out so late.

   The game has always been played regardless of the weather.

2. No verb preceded by *to* is ever the verb of a sentence.

   Sue wants to go with us.

   The newly married couple decided to rent a house for a year.

   The store needs extra people to help out at Christmas.

3. No *-ing* word by itself is ever the verb of a sentence. (It may be part of the verb, but it must have a helping verb in front of it.)

   We planning the trip for months. (This is not a sentence, because the verb is not complete.)

   We were planning the trip for months. (This is a complete sentence.)

Practice

5

Draw a single line under subjects and a double line under verbs. Be sure to include all parts of the verb.

1. He has been sleeping all day.

2. The wood foundations of the shed were attacked by termites.

3. I have not washed my car for several months.

4. The instructor had not warned us about the quiz.

5. The bus will be leaving shortly.

6. You should not try to pet that temperamental hamster.

7. They have just been married by a justice of the peace.

8. He could make a living with his wood carvings.

9. Kim has decided to ask her boss for a raise.

10. The employees should have warned us about the wet floor.

Compound Subjects and Verbs

A sentence may have more than one verb:

The dancer stumbled and fell.

Lola washed her hair, blew it dry, and parted it in the middle.

A sentence may have more than one subject:

Cats and dogs are sometimes the best of friends.

The striking workers and their bosses could not come to an agreement.

A sentence may have several subjects and several verbs:

Holly and I read the book and reported on it to the class.

Pete, Nick, and Eric caught the fish in the morning, cleaned them in the after-

noon, and ate them that night.

Draw a single line under subjects and a double line under verbs. Be sure to mark
all the subjects and verbs.

Practice

6

1. The hypnotist locked his assistant in a box and sawed her in half.

2. Trina began her paper at 7:30 and finished it at midnight.

3. On the shipping pier, the Nissans, Toyotas, and Hondas glittered in the sun.

4. Tony added the column of figures three times and got three different totals.

5. The car sputtered, stalled, and then started again.

6. Whiteflies, mites, and aphids infected my houseplants.

7. Rosa disconnected the computers and carried them to her car.

8. We walked over to the corner deli and bought extra cheese for the party.

9. At the new shopping mall, Tony and Lola looked in windows for two hours

   and then bought one pair of socks.

10. My aunt and uncle married in their twenties, divorced in their thirties, and

    then remarried in their forties.

Review Test 1

Draw one line under the subjects and two lines under the verbs. As necessary, cross out prepositional phrases to help find subjects. Underline all the parts of a verb. And remember that you may find more than one subject and verb in a sentence.

1. I had not heard about the cancellation of the class.

2. James should have gotten an estimate from the plumber.

3. The family played badminton and volleyball at the picnic.

4. A solution to the problem popped suddenly into my head.

5. My roommate and I will need to study all night for the test.

6. Chang has not been eating in the cafeteria this semester.

7. The white moon hung above the castle like a grinning skull.

8. Len and Marie drove all night and arrived at their vacation cottage early Saturday morning.

9. The game has been postponed because of bad weather and will be rescheduled for later in the season.

10. The sun reflected sharply off the lake and forced me to wear sunglasses.

Review Test 2

Follow the directions given for Review Test 1.

1. The doctors were speaking gently to the parents of the little girl.

2. A rumor has been spreading about the possible closing of the plant.

3. Diesel trucks with heavy exhaust fumes should be banned from the road.

4. The dental assistant should have warned me about the pain.

5. With their fingers, the children started to draw pictures on the steamed window.

6. Three buildings down the street from my house have been demolished.

7. Rats, squirrels, and bats lived in the attic of the abandoned house.

8. Jack and Bob will be anchoring the long-distance team in the track meet.

9. Reluctantly, I crawled from my bed and stumbled to the bathroom.

10. Tiddlywinks, pickup sticks, and hearts were our favorite childhood games.

Fragments

5

Introductory Activity

Every sentence must have a subject and a verb and must express a complete thought. A word group that lacks a subject or a verb and that does not express a complete thought is a *fragment*.

Listed below are a number of fragments and sentences. See if you can complete the statement that explains each fragment.

1. Teapots. *Fragment*

   Teapots whistled. *Sentence*

   "Teapots" is a fragment because, while it has a subject (*Teapots*), it lacks

   a _____ (*whistled*) and so does not express a complete thought.

2. Instructs. *Fragment*

   Quincy instructs. *Sentence*

   "Instructs" is a fragment because, while it has a verb (*Instructs*), it lacks

   a _____ (*Quincy*) and does not express a complete thought.

3. Discussing homework in class. *Fragment*

   Ellie was discussing homework in class. *Sentence*

   "Discussing homework in class" is a fragment because it lacks a

   _____ (*Ellie*) and also part of the _____ (*was*). As a result,

   it does not express a complete thought.

continued

4. When my mother began lecturing me.   *Fragment*

    When my mother began lecturing me, I rolled my eyes.   *Sentence*

"When my mother began lecturing me" is a fragment because we want to know *what happened when* the mother began lecturing. The word group does not follow through and express a complete _____.

Answers are on page 559.

What Fragments Are

Every sentence must have a subject and a verb and must express a complete thought. A word group that lacks a subject or a verb and does not express a complete thought is a *fragment*. Following are the most common types of fragments that people write:

1. Dependent-word fragments

2. *-ing* and *to* fragments

3. Added-detail fragments

4. Missing-subject fragments

Once you understand the specific kind or kinds of fragments that you might write, you should be able to eliminate them from your writing. The following pages explain all four types of fragments.

Dependent-Word Fragments

Some word groups that begin with a dependent word are fragments. Here is a list of common dependent words:

Common Dependent Words	
after	unless
although, though	until
as	what, whatever
because	when, whenever
before	where, wherever
even though	whether
how	which, whichever
if, even if	while
in order that	who
since	whose
that, so that	

Whenever you start a sentence with one of these dependent words, you must be careful that a dependent-word fragment does not result. The word group beginning with the dependent word *after* in the selection below is a fragment.

After I stopped drinking coffee. I began sleeping better at night.

A *dependent statement*—one starting with a dependent word like *after*—cannot stand alone. It depends on another statement to complete the thought. "After I stopped drinking coffee" is a dependent statement. It leaves us hanging. We expect in the same sentence to find out *what happened after* the writer stopped drinking coffee. When a writer does not follow through and complete a thought, a fragment results. To correct the fragment, follow through and complete the thought:

After I stopped drinking coffee, I began sleeping better at night.

Remember, then, that *dependent statements by themselves* are fragments. They must be attached to a statement that makes sense standing alone.* Here are two other examples of dependent-word fragments.

Brian sat nervously in the dental clinic. While waiting to have his wisdom tooth pulled.

Maria decided to throw away the boxes. That had accumulated for years in the basement.

"While waiting to have his wisdom tooth pulled" is a fragment; it does not make sense standing by itself. We want to know in the same statement *what Brian did* while waiting to have his tooth pulled. The writer must complete the thought. Likewise, "That had accumulated for years in the basement" is not in itself a complete thought. We want to know in the same statement what *that* refers to.

How to | Correct Dependent-Word Fragments

In most cases, you can correct a dependent-word fragment by attaching it to the sentence that comes after it or to the sentence that comes before it:

After I stopped drinking coffee, I began sleeping better at night. (The fragment has been attached to the sentence that comes after it.)

Brian sat nervously in the dental clinic while waiting to have his wisdom tooth pulled. (The fragment has been attached to the sentence that comes before it.)

continued

---

*Some instructors refer to a dependent-word fragment as a *dependent clause*. A *clause* is simply a group of words having a subject and a verb. A clause may be *independent* (expressing a complete thought and able to stand alone) or *dependent* (not expressing a complete thought and not able to stand alone). A dependent clause by itself is a fragment. It can be corrected simply by adding an independent clause.

Maria decided to throw away the boxes that had accumulated for years in the basement. (The fragment has been attached to the sentence that comes before it.)

Another way of correcting a dependent-word fragment is to eliminate the dependent word and make a new sentence:

I stopped drinking coffee.

He was waiting to have his wisdom tooth pulled.

They had accumulated for years in the basement.

Do not use the second method of correction too frequently, however, for it may cut down on interest and variety in your writing style.

TIPS

1. Use a comma if a dependent-word group comes at the *beginning* of a sentence (see also page 357):

   After I stopped drinking coffee, I began sleeping better at night.

   However, do not generally use a comma if the dependent-word group comes at the end of a sentence:

   Brian sat nervously in the dental clinic while waiting to have his wisdom tooth pulled.

   Maria decided to throw away the boxes that had accumulated for years in the basement.

2. Sometimes the dependent words *who, that, which,* or *where* appear not at the very start but *near* the start of a word group. A fragment often results.

   Today I visited Hilda Cooper. A friend who is in the hospital.

   "A friend who is in the hospital" is not in itself a complete thought. We want to know in the same statement *who* the friend is. The fragment can be corrected by attaching it to the sentence that comes before it:

   Today I visited Hilda Cooper, a friend who is in the hospital.

   (Here a comma is used to set off "a friend who is in the hospital," which is extra material placed at the end of the sentence.)

Practice

1

Turn each of the dependent-word groups into a sentence by adding a complete thought. Put a comma after the dependent-word group if a dependent word starts the sentence.

3. Noah picked through the box of chocolates. Removing the kinds he didn't like. He saved these for his wife and ate the rest.

_____

_____

4. The grass I was walking on suddenly became squishy. Having hiked into a marsh of some kind.

Having I hiked into a marsh of some kind.

_____

5. Steve drove quickly to the bank. To cash his paycheck. Otherwise, he would have had no money for the weekend.

_____

_____

_____

Added-Detail Fragments

Added-detail fragments lack a subject and a verb. They often begin with one of the following words or phrases.

also	**except**	**including**
especially	**for example**	**such as**

See if you can underline the one added-detail fragment in each of these examples:

Example 1

Tony has trouble accepting criticism. Except from Lola. She has a knack for tact.

Example 2

My apartment has its drawbacks. For example, no hot water in the morning.

Example 3

I had many jobs while in school. Among them, busboy, painter, and security guard.

People often write added-detail fragments for much the same reason they write -*ing* fragments. They think the subject and verb in one sentence will serve for the next word group as well. But the subject and verb must be in *each* word group.

How to Correct Added-Detail Fragments

1. Attach the fragment to the complete thought that precedes it. Example 1 could read, "Tony has trouble accepting criticism, except from Lola." (Note that here a comma is used to set off "except from Lola," which is extra material placed at the end of the sentence.)

2. Add a subject and a verb to the fragment to make it a complete sentence. Example 2 could read, "My apartment has its drawbacks. For example, there is no hot water in the morning."

3. Change words as necessary to make the fragment part of the preceding sentence. Example 3 could read, "Among the many jobs I had while in school were busboy, painter, and security guard."

Practice

5

Underline the fragment in each selection below. Then make it a sentence by rewriting it, using the method described in parentheses.

EXAMPLE

My husband and I share the household chores. <u>Including meals.</u> I do the cooking and he does the eating.
(Add the fragment to the preceding sentence.)

My husband and I share the household chores, including meals.

1. Hakeem is very accident-prone. For example, managing to cut his hand while crumbling a bar of shredded wheat.
   (Correct the fragment by adding the subject *he* and changing *managing* to *managed*.)

   For example, he managed to cut his hand while crumbling a bar of shredded wheat

2. Tina's job in the customer service department depressed her. All day, people complained. About missing parts, rude salespeople, and errors on bills.
   (Add the fragment to the preceding sentence.)

   _____

   _____

3. My mother is always giving me household hints. For example, using club
    soda on stains. Unfortunately, I never remember them.
    (Correct the fragment by adding the subject and verb *she suggests*.)

    For example, she suggest using club
    soda on stains.

Underline the added-detail fragment in each selection. Then rewrite that part of
the selection needed to correct the fragment. Use one of the three methods of correction described on page 88.

Practice

6

1. My little boy is constantly into mischief. Such as tearing the labels off all
    the cans in the cupboard.

    _____

    _____

2. The old house was filled with expensive woodwork. For example, a hand-
    carved mantel and a mahogany banister.

    _____

    _____

3. Andy used to have many bad eating habits. For instance, chewing with his
    mouth open.

    For instance, he chewed with his
    mouth open.

4. I put potatoes in the oven without first punching holes in them. A half hour
    later, there were several explosions. With potatoes splattering all over the
    walls of the oven.

    _____

    _____

5. Janet looked forward to seeing former classmates at the high school reunion.
    Including the football player she had had a wild crush on. She wondered if
    he had grown fat and bald.

    _____

    _____

Missing-Subject Fragments

In each example below, underline the word group in which the subject is missing.

Example 1

One example of my father's generosity is that he visits sick friends in the hospital. And takes along get-well cards with a few dollars folded in them.

Example 2

The weight lifter grunted as he heaved the barbells into the air. Then, with a loud groan, dropped them.

People write missing-subject fragments because they think the subject in one sentence will apply to the next word group as well. But the subject, as well as the verb, must be in *each* word group to make it a sentence.

How to   Correct Missing-Subject Fragments

1. Attach the fragment to the preceding sentence. Example 1 could read, "One illustration of my father's generosity is that he visits sick friends in the hospital and takes along get-well cards with a few dollars folded in them."

2. Add a subject (which can often be a pronoun standing for the subject in the preceding sentence). Example 2 could read, "Then, with a loud groan, he dropped them."

Practice

7

Underline the missing-subject fragment in each selection. Then rewrite that part of the selection needed to correct the fragment. Use one of the two methods of correction described above.

1. Fred went to the refrigerator to get milk for his breakfast cereal. And discovered about one tablespoon of milk left in the carton.

   And he discovered _____

   _____

2. At the laundromat, I loaded the dryer with wet clothes. Then noticed the "Out of Order" sign taped over the coin slot.

   Then I noticed _____

   _____

3. Our neighborhood's most eligible bachelor got married this weekend. But did not invite us to the <u>wedding</u>. We all wondered what the bride was like.

   But he did not

4. Larry's father could not accept his son's lifestyle. Also, was constantly criticizing Larry's choice of friends.

   Also, he was

5. Wanda stared at the blank page in desperation. And decided that the first sentence of a paper is always the hardest to write.

   And she decided

www.mhhe.com/langan

A REVIEW

How to Check for Fragments

1. Read your paper aloud from the *last* sentence to the *first*. You will be better able to see and hear whether each word group you read is a complete thought.

2. If you think any word group is a fragment, ask yourself, Does this contain a subject and a verb and express a complete thought?

3. More specifically, be on the lookout for the most common fragments.

   • Dependent-word fragments (starting with words like *after, because, since, when,* and *before*)

   • *-ing* and *to* fragments (*-ing* or *to* at or near the start of a word group)

   • Added-detail fragments (starting with words like *for example, such as, also,* and *especially*)

   • Missing-subject fragments (a verb is present but not the subject)

Collaborative Activity

Editing and Rewriting

Working with a partner, read the short paragraph below and underline the five fragments. Then correct the fragments. Feel free to discuss the rewrite quietly with your partner and refer back to the chapter when necessary.

¹I am only thirty, but a trip to the movies recently made me realize that my youth is definitely past. ²The science-fiction movie had attracted a large audience of younger kids and teenagers. ³Before the movie began. ⁴Groups of kids ran up and down the aisles, laughing, giggling, and spilling popcorn. ⁵I was annoyed with them. ⁶But thought, "At one time I was doing the same thing. ⁷Now I'm acting like one of the adults." ⁸The thought was a little depressing, for I remembered how much fun it was not to care what the adults thought. ⁹Soon after the movie began, a group of teenagers walked in and sat in the first row. ¹⁰During the movie, they vied with each other. ¹¹To see who could make the loudest comment. ¹²Or the most embarrassing noise. ¹³Some of the adults in the theater complained to the usher, but I had a guilty memory about doing the same thing myself a few times. ¹⁴In addition, a teenage couple was sitting in front of me. ¹⁵Occasionally, these two held hands or the boy put his arm around the girl. ¹⁶A few times, they sneaked a kiss. ¹⁷Realizing that my wife and I were long past this kind of behavior in the movies. ¹⁸I again felt like an old man.

Collaborative Activity

Creating Sentences

Working with a partner, make up your own short fragments test as directed. Write one or more of your sentences about the photo shown here.

1. Write a dependent-word fragment in the space below. Then correct the fragment by making it into a complete sentence. You may want to begin your fragment with the word *before, after, when, because,* or *if.*

   Fragment _____

   Sentence _____

   _____

2. Write a fragment that begins with a word that has an *-ing* ending in the space below. Then correct the fragment by making it into a complete sentence. You may want to begin your fragment with the word *laughing, walking, shopping,* or *talking.*

   Fragment _____

   Sentence _____

   _____

3. Write an added-detail fragment in the space below. Then correct the fragment by making it into a complete sentence. You may want to begin your fragment with the word *also, especially, except,* or *including.*

   Fragment _____

   Sentence _____

   _____

Reflective Activity

1. Look at the paragraph about going to the movies that you revised. How has removing fragments affected the reading of the paragraph? Explain.

2. Explain what it is about fragments that you find most difficult to remember and apply. Use an example to make your point clear. Feel free to refer to anything in this chapter.

Review Test 1

Turn each of the following word groups into a complete sentence. Use the space provided.

EXAMPLES

Feeling very confident

Feeling very confident, I began my speech.

Until the rain started

We played softball until the rain started.

1. Before you sit down

   _____

2. When the noise stopped

   _____

3. To get to the game on time

   _____

4. During my walk along the trail

   _____

5. Because I was short on cash

   _____

6. Lucy, whom I know well

   _____

Run-Ons

6

Introductory Activity

A run-on occurs when two sentences are run together with no adequate sign given to mark the break between them. Shown below are four run-on sentences and four correctly marked sentences. See if you can complete the statement that explains how each run-on is corrected.

1. A student yawned in class the result was a chain reaction of copycat yawning.

   A student yawned in class. The result was a chain reaction of copycat yawning.

The run-on has been corrected by using a _____ and a capital letter to separate the two complete thoughts.

2. I placed an ad in the paper last week, no one has replied.

   I placed an ad in the paper last week, but no one has replied.

The run-on has been corrected by using a joining word, _____, to connect the two complete thoughts.

3. A bus barreled down the street, it splashed murky rainwater all over the pedestrians.

   A bus barreled down the street; it splashed murky rainwater all over the pedestrians.

continued

The run-on has been corrected by using a _____ to connect the two closely related thoughts.

4. I had a campus map, I still could not find my classroom building.

Although I had a campus map, I still could not find my classroom building.

The run-on has been corrected by using the dependent word _____ to connect the two closely related thoughts.

Answers are on page 560.

www.mhhe.com/langan

What Are Run-Ons?

A *run-on* is two complete thoughts that are run together with no adequate sign given to mark the break between them. As a result of the run-on, the reader is confused, unsure of where one thought ends and the next one begins. Two types of run-ons are fused sentences and comma splices.

Some run-ons have no punctuation at all to mark the break between the thoughts. Such run-ons are known as *fused sentences:* they are fused or joined together as if they were only one thought.

Fused Sentence
Rosa decided to stop smoking she didn't want to die of lung cancer.

Fused Sentence
The exam was postponed the class was canceled as well.

In other run-ons, known as *comma splices,* a comma is used to connect or "splice" together the two complete thoughts.* However, a comma alone is *not enough* to connect two complete thoughts. Some connection stronger than a comma alone is needed.

Notes:
1. Some instructors feel that the term *run-ons* should be applied only to fused sentences, not to comma splices. But for many other instructors, and for our purposes in this book, the term *run-on* applies equally to fused sentences and comma splices. The bottom line is that you do not want either fused sentences or comma splices in your writing.
2. Some instructors refer to each complete thought in a run-on as an *independent clause.* A *clause* is simply a group of words having a subject and a verb. A clause may be *independent* (expressing a complete thought and able to stand alone) or *dependent* (not expressing a complete thought and not able to stand alone). A run-on is two independent clauses that are run together with no adequate sign given to mark the break between them.

Comma Splice

Rosa decided to stop smoking, she didn't want to die of lung cancer.

Comma Splice

The exam was postponed, the class was canceled as well.

Comma splices are the most common kind of run-on. Students sense that some kind of connection is needed between thoughts, and so they put a comma at the dividing point. But the comma alone is *not sufficient.* A stronger, clearer mark is needed between the two thoughts.

A Warning: Words That Can Lead to Run-Ons

People often write run-ons when the second complete thought begins with one of the following words:

I	**we**	**there**	**now**
you	**they**	**this**	**then**
he, she, it		**that**	**next**

Remember to be on the alert for run-ons whenever you use these words in your writing.

Correcting Run-Ons

Here are four common methods of correcting a run-on:

1. Use a period and a capital letter to separate the two complete thoughts. (In other words, make two separate sentences of the two complete thoughts.)

   Rosa decided to stop smoking. She didn't want to die of lung cancer.

   The exam was postponed. The class was canceled as well.

2. Use a comma plus a joining word (*and, but, for, or, nor, so, yet*) to connect the two complete thoughts.

   Rosa decided to stop smoking, for she didn't want to die of lung cancer.

   The exam was postponed, and the class was canceled as well.

3. Use a semicolon to connect the two complete thoughts.

   Rosa decided to stop smoking; she didn't want to die of lung cancer.

   The exam was postponed; the class was canceled as well.

continued

> 4. Use subordination (put a dependent word at the beginning of one fragment).
>
>   Because Rosa didn't want to die of lung cancer, she decided to stop smoking.
>
>   When the exam was postponed, the class was canceled as well.

The following pages will give you practice in all four methods of correcting run-ons. The use of subordination will be explained further on page 133, in a chapter that deals with sentence variety.

Method 1: Period and a Capital Letter

One way of correcting a run-on is to use a period and a capital letter at the break between the two complete thoughts. Use this method especially if the thoughts are not closely related or if another method would make the sentence too long.

Practice

1

Locate the split in each of the following run-ons. Each is a *fused sentence*—that is, each consists of two sentences fused or joined together with no punctuation at all between them. Reading each sentence aloud will help you "hear" where a major break or split in the thought occurs. At such a point, your voice will probably drop and pause.

Correct the run-on by putting a period at the end of the first thought and a capital letter at the start of the second thought.

EXAMPLE

Gary was not a success at his job. his mouth moved faster than his hands. *(H above "his")*

1. Gerald's motorized wheelchair broke down he was unable to go to class.

2. The subway train hurtled through the station a blur of spray paint and graffiti flashed in front of my eyes.

3. Jenny panicked the car had stalled on a treacherous traffic circle.

4. Half the class flunked the exam the other half of the students were absent.

5. One reason for the high cost of new furniture is the cost of good wood one walnut tree sold recently for $40,000.

6. The wedding reception began to get out of hand guests started to throw cake at each other.

7. Jamal's pitchfork turned over the rich earth earthworms poked their heads out of new furrows.

instead of *for* in the activities that follow. If you do use *because,* omit the comma before it.

SO   as a result, therefore

Our son misbehaved again, so he was sent upstairs without dessert.

(*So* means *as a result:* Our son misbehaved again; *as a result,* he was sent upstairs without dessert.)

Insert the comma and the joining word (*and, but, for, so*) that logically connects the two thoughts in each sentence.

EXAMPLE

A trip to the zoo always depresses me, *for* I hate to see animals in cages.

1. The telephone was ringing someone was at the front door as well.

2. Something was obviously wrong with the meat loaf it was glowing in the dark.

3. Tia and Nina enjoyed the movie they wished the seats had been more comfortable.

4. Brett moved from Boston to Los Angeles he wanted to get as far away as possible from his ex-wife.

5. I decided to go back to school I felt my brain was turning to slush.

6. Lola loved the rose cashmere sweater she had nothing to wear with it.

7. Art's son has joined the Army his daughter is thinking of joining, too.

8. Lydia began working the second shift she is not able to eat supper with her family anymore.

9. Fred remembered to get the hamburger he forgot to buy the hamburger rolls.

10. My TV wasn't working I walked over to a friend's house to watch the game.

Practice

5

Add a complete, closely related thought to each of the following statements. When you write the second thought, use a comma plus the joining word shown at the left.

EXAMPLE

but I was sick with the flu, *but I still had to study for the test.*

so 1. The night was hot and humid _____

_____

but 2. Fred wanted to get a pizza _____

_____

and 3. Lola went shopping in the morning _____

_____

for 4. I'm going to sell my car _____

_____

but 5. I expected the exam to be easy _____

_____

Method 3: Semicolon

A third method of correcting a run-on is to use a semicolon to mark the break between two thoughts. A *semicolon* (;) is made up of a period above a comma and is sometimes called a *strong comma*. The semicolon signals more of a pause than a comma alone but not quite the full pause of a period.

Occasional use of semicolons can add variety to sentences. For some people, however, the semicolon is a confusing mark of punctuation. Keep in mind that if you are not comfortable using it, you can and should use one of the first two methods of correcting a run-on sentence.

Semicolon Alone

Here are some earlier sentences that were connected with a comma plus a joining word. Now they are connected with a semicolon. Notice that a semicolon, unlike a comma, can be used alone to connect the two complete thoughts in each sentence.

Natalie was watching Monday night football; she was doing her homework as well.

I voted for the president two years ago; I would not vote for him today.

Saturday is the worst day to shop; people jam the stores.

Insert a semicolon where the break occurs between the two complete thoughts in each of the following sentences.

EXAMPLE

She had a wig on; it looked more like a hat than a wig.

1. I just canceled my cell phone service the bill was just too expensive.

2. Reggie wanted to watch *American Idol* the rest of the family insisted on watching a movie.

3. Bonnie put a freshly baked batch of chocolate chip cookies on the counter to cool everyone gathered round for samples.

4. About $25 million worth of pizza is eaten each year an average of three hundred new pizza parlors open every week.

5. Nate never heard the third base coach screaming for him to stop he was out at home plate by ten feet.

Semicolon with a Transition

A semicolon is sometimes used with a transitional word and a comma to join two complete thoughts:

I figured that the ball game would cost me about ten dollars; however, I didn't consider the high price of food and drinks.

Fred and Martha have a low-interest mortgage on their house; otherwise, they would move to another neighborhood.

Sharon didn't understand the instructor's point; therefore, she asked him to repeat it.

TIP Sometimes transitional words do not join complete thoughts but are merely interrupters in a sentence (see pages 358–359):

My parents, moreover, plan to go on the trip.
I believe, however, that they'll change their minds.

Transitional Words

Here is a list of common transitional words (also called *adverbial conjunctions*).

Common Transitional Words		
however	moreover	therefore
on the other hand	in addition	as a result
nevertheless	also	consequently
instead	furthermore	otherwise

Practice

7

For each item, choose a logical transitional word from the box above and write it in the space provided. In addition, put a semicolon *before* the transition and a comma *after* it.

EXAMPLE

It was raining harder than ever ___; however,___ Bobby was determined to go to the amusement park.

1. The tree must be sprayed with insecticide _____ the spider mites will kill it.

2. I helped the magician set up his props _____ I agreed to let him saw me in half.

3. Fred never finished paneling his basement _____ he hired a carpenter to complete the job.

4. My house was robbed last week _____ I bought a watchdog.

5. Juanita is taking five courses this semester _____ she is working forty hours a week.

Practice

8

Punctuate each sentence by using a semicolon and a comma.

EXAMPLE

Our tap water has a funny taste;consequently,we buy bottled water to drink.

1. I arrived early to get a good seat however there were already a hundred people outside the door.

2. Foul language marred the live boxing match as a result next time the network will probably use a tape delay.

3. The fluorescent lights in the library gave Jan a headache furthermore they distracted her by making a loud humming sound.

4.   The broken shells on the beach were like tiny razors consequently we walked along with extreme caution.

5.   Ted carefully combed and recombed his hair nevertheless his bald spot still showed.

Method 4: Subordination

A fourth method of joining related thoughts is to use subordination. *Subordination* is a way of showing that one thought in a sentence is not as important as another thought. Here are three sentences in which one idea is subordinated to (made less emphatic than) the other idea:

> Because Rosa didn't want to die of lung cancer, she decided to stop smoking.
>
> The wedding reception began to get out of hand when the guests started to throw food at each other.
>
> Although my brothers wanted to watch a *Star Trek* rerun, the rest of the family insisted on turning to the network news.

Dependent Words

Notice that when we subordinate, we use dependent words like *because, when,* and *although.* Following is a brief list of common dependent words (see the complete list on page 128). Subordination is explained in full on pages 133–134.

Common Dependent Words		
after	before	unless
although	even though	until
as	if	when
because	since	while

Choose a logical dependent word from the box above and write it in the space provided.

EXAMPLE

Although going up a ladder is easy, looking down can be difficult.

1.   The instructor is lowering my grade in the course _____ I was late for class three times.

2.   _____ the airplane dropped a few feet, my stomach rose a few feet.

3.   _____ the football game was being played, we sent out for a pizza.

4.   _____ the football game was over, we went out for another pizza.

5.   You should talk to a counselor _____ you decide on your courses for next semester.

Practice

9

Practice

10

Rewrite the five sentences below, taken from this chapter, so that one idea is subordinate to the other. In each case, use one of the dependent words in the box on page 113.

EXAMPLE

My house was burglarized last week; I bought a watchdog.

Because my house was burglarized last week, I bought a watchdog.

> **HINT** As in the example, use a comma if a dependent statement starts a sentence.

1. Sharon didn't understand the instructor's point; she asked him to repeat it.

   _____

   _____

2. Marco remembered to get the hamburger; he forgot to get the hamburger rolls.

   _____

   _____

3. Michael gulped two cups of strong coffee; his heart started to flutter.

   _____

   _____

4. A car sped around the corner; it sprayed slush all over the pedestrians.

   _____

   _____

5. Lola loved the rose cashmere sweater; she had nothing to wear with it.

   _____

   _____

Collaborative Activity

Editing and Rewriting

Working with a partner, read carefully the short paragraph below and underline the five run-ons. Then use the space provided to correct the five run-ons. Feel free to discuss the rewrite quietly with your partner and refer back to the chapter when necessary.

[1]When Mark began his first full-time job, he immediately got a credit card, a used sports car was his first purchase. [2]Then he began to buy expensive clothes that he could not afford he also bought impressive gifts for his parents and his girlfriend. [3]Several months passed before Mark realized that he owed an enormous amount of money. [4]To make matters worse, his car broke down, a stack of bills suddenly seemed to be due at once. [5]Mark tried to cut back on his purchases, he soon realized he had to cut up his credit card to prevent himself from using it. [6]He also began keeping a careful record of his spending he had no idea where his money had gone till then. [7]He hated to admit to his family and friends that he had to get his budget under control. [8]However, his girlfriend said she did not mind inexpensive dates, and his parents were proud of his growing maturity.

_____

_____

_____

_____

_____

_____

_____

_____

Collaborative Activity

Creating Sentences

Working with a partner, make up your own short run-ons test as directed.

1. Write a run-on sentence. Then rewrite it, using a period and capital letter to separate the thoughts into two sentences.

    Run-on _____

    _____

    Rewrite _____

    _____

2. Write a sentence that has two complete thoughts. Then rewrite it, using a comma and a joining word to correctly join the complete thoughts.

    Two complete thoughts _____

    _____

    Rewrite _____

    _____

3. Write a sentence that has two complete thoughts. Then rewrite it, using a semicolon to correctly join the complete thoughts.

    Two complete thoughts _____

    _____

    Rewrite _____

    _____

Reflective Activity

1. Look at the paragraph about Mark that you revised above. Explain how run-ons interfere with your reading of the paragraph.

2. In your own written work, which type of run-on are you most likely to write: comma splices or fused sentences? Why do you tend to make the kind of mistake that you do?

3. Which method for correcting run-ons are you most likely to use in your own writing? Which are you least likely to use? Why?

Review Test 1

Some of the run-ons that follow are *fused sentences,* having no punctuation between the two complete thoughts; others are *comma splices,* having only a comma between the two complete thoughts.

Correct the run-ons by using one of the following three methods:

- Period and a capital letter
- Comma and a joining word (*and, but, for, so*)
- Semicolon

Use whichever method seems most appropriate in each case.

EXAMPLE

Fred pulled the cellophane off the cake, *and* the icing came along with it.

1. I found the cat sleeping on the stove the dog was eating the morning mail.

2. Yoko has a twenty-mile drive to school she sometimes arrives late for class.

3. I lifted the empty water bottle above me a few more drops fell out of it and into my thirsty mouth.

4. These pants are guaranteed to wear like iron they also feel like iron.

5. I saw a black-and-white blob on the highway soon the odor of skunk wafted through my car.

6. She gets A's in her math homework by using her pocket calculator she is not allowed to use the calculator at school.

7. Flies were getting into the house the window screen was torn.

8. Martha moans and groans upon getting up in the morning she sounds like a crazy woman.

9. Lola met Tony at McDonald's they shared a large order of fries.

10. The carpet in their house needs to be replaced the walls should be painted as well.

Review Test 2

Correct the run-on in each sentence by using subordination. Choose from among the following dependent words.

after	before	unless
although	even though	until
as	if	when
because	since	while

EXAMPLE

Tony hated going to a new barber, he was afraid his hair would be butchered.

Because Tony was afraid his hair would be butchered, he hated going to a new barber.

1. The meal and conversation were enjoyable, I kept worrying about the check.

   _____

   _____

2. My wet fingers stuck to the frosty ice cube tray, I had to pry them loose.

   _____

   _____

3. I take a late afternoon nap, my mind and body are refreshed and ready for my night course.

   _____

   _____

4. Our daughter jumped up screaming a black spider was on her leg.

   _____

   _____

5. I wanted badly to cry I remained cold and silent.

   _____

   _____

NAME: _____

DATE: _____

Run-Ons   MASTERY TEST 4

In the space provided, write *R-O* beside run-on sentences. Write *C* beside the one sentence that is punctuated correctly. Some of the run-ons have no punctuation between the two complete thoughts; others have only a comma.

Correct each run-on by using (1) a period and capital letter, (2) a comma and a joining word, or (3) a semicolon. Do not use the same method of correction for every sentence.

_____   1. The supermarket needs to hire more cashiers customers must stand in long checkout lines just to buy a few groceries.

_____   2. The news reporter said the snowstorm would dump a foot of snow on our city, but all we saw were a few flurries.

_____   3. Metal detectors are being installed in many high schools this will prevent students from bringing weapons to school.

_____   4. Critics said the new movie was horrible the large crowd in the theater seemed to disagree.

_____   5. Dust and cat fur covered the floor of the old attic it was an allergy sufferer's nightmare.

_____   6. Kendra looked everywhere for her car keys they turned out to be in her pocket.

_____   7. Honeybees can communicate to each other by "dancing" their movements tell other bees where to find nectar-filled flowers.

_____   8. The volcano destroyed the surrounding forest thousands of old trees were snapped like dry twigs.

_____   9. Ken's new dog has a bad habit it likes to eat leather shoes.

_____   10. Leeches are unpleasant wormlike creatures that drink blood they can also help doctors treat severe injuries.

NAME: _____

DATE: _____

MASTERY TEST 5 Run-Ons

In the space provided, write *R-O* beside run-on sentences. Write *C* beside the one sentence that is punctuated correctly. Some of the run-ons have no punctuation between the two complete thoughts; others have only a comma.

Correct each run-on by using (1) a period and a capital letter, (2) a comma and a joining word, or (3) a semicolon. Do not use the same method of correction for every sentence.

_____ 1. The cable company increased rates twice this year customers have threatened to cancel their service.

_____ 2. Bill wanted to arrive for the interview early he missed his bus.

_____ 3. The salesperson said the used car was in perfect shape the engine was dotted with rust.

_____ 4. Wind howled through the trees rain pelted loudly against the windows of our house.

_____ 5. A pen exploded in the washing machine all Sara's clothes were stained in blue ink.

_____ 6. In the 1300s, one-third of Europe's population was killed by the bubonic plague this highly contagious disease was spread by fleas.

_____ 7. Kathy spilled soda on her expensive new cell phone, and then it stopped working.

_____ 8. Angry basketball fans yelled at the referee his mistakes cost the team at least six points.

_____ 9. Security cameras filmed the jewelry store robbery police have not been able to catch the thieves.

_____ 10. Today, the average American woman can expect to live seventy-nine years the lifespan of the average man is just seventy-five.

Sentence Variety I

This chapter will show you how to write effective and varied sentences. You'll learn more about two techniques—subordination and coordination—you can use to expand simple sentences, making them more interesting and expressive. You'll also reinforce what you have learned in Chapters 5 and 6 about how subordination and coordination can help you correct fragments and run-ons in your writing.

Four Traditional Sentence Patterns

Sentences in English are traditionally described as *simple, compound, complex,* or *compound-complex.* Each is explained below.

The Simple Sentence

A simple sentence has a single subject-verb combination.

Children play.

The game ended early.

My car stalled three times last week.

The lake has been polluted by several neighboring streams.

A simple sentence may have more than one subject:

Lola and Tony drove home.

The wind and water dried my hair.

or more than one verb:

> The <u>children</u> <u>smiled</u> and <u>waved</u> at us.

> The <u>lawn mower</u> <u>smoked</u> and <u>sputtered</u>.

or several subjects and verbs:

> <u>Manny</u>, <u>Moe</u>, and <u>Jack</u> <u>lubricated</u> my car, <u>replaced</u> the oil filter, and <u>cleaned</u> the spark plugs.

Practice

1

On separate paper, write:

> Three sentences, each with a single subject and verb

> Three sentences, each with a single subject and a double verb

> Three sentences, each with a double subject and a single verb

In each case, underline the subject once and the verb twice. (See pages 67–68 if necessary for more information on subjects and verbs.)

The Compound Sentence

A compound, or "double," sentence is made up of two (or more) simple sentences. The two complete statements in a compound sentence are usually connected by a comma plus a joining word (*and, but, for, or, nor, so, yet*).

A compound sentence is used when you want to give equal weight to two closely related ideas. The technique of showing that ideas have equal importance is called *coordination*.

Following are some compound sentences. Each sentence contains two ideas that the writer considers equal in importance.

> The rain increased, so the officials canceled the game.

> Martha wanted to go shopping, but Fred refused to drive her.

> Hollis was watching television in the family room, and April was upstairs on the phone.

> I had to give up woodcarving, for my arthritis had become very painful.

4. _____ I have lived all my life on the East Coast, I felt
   uncomfortable during a West Coast vacation, _____ I kept
   thinking that the ocean was on the wrong side.

5. _____ water condensation continues in your basement, either
   you should buy a dehumidifier _____ you should cover
   the masonry walls with waterproof paint.

On separate paper, write five compound-complex sentences.

Practice

9

Review of Subordination and Coordination

Subordination and coordination are ways of showing the exact relationship of
ideas within a sentence. Through **subordination** we show that one idea is less
important than another. When we subordinate, we use dependent words like *when,*
although, while, because, and *after*. (A list of common dependent words has been
given on page 128.) Through **coordination** we show that ideas are of equal importance. When we coordinate, we use the words *and, but, for, or, nor, so, yet*.

www.mhhe.com/langan

Use subordination or coordination to combine the following groups of simple sentences into one or more longer sentences. Be sure to omit repeated words. Since
various combinations are possible, you might want to jot down several combinations
on separate paper. Then read them aloud to find the combination that sounds best.
    Keep in mind that, very often, the relationship among ideas in a sentence will
be clearer when subordination rather than coordination is used.

Practice

10

EXAMPLE

- My car does not start on cold mornings.
- I think the battery needs to be replaced.
- I already had it recharged once.
- I don't think charging it again would help.

Because my car does not start on cold mornings, I think the battery

needs to be replaced. I already had it recharged once, so I don't think

charging it again would help.

> **COMMA HINTS**
>
> a. Use a comma at the end of a word group that starts with a dependent word (as in "Because my car does not start on cold mornings, . . .").
>
> b. Use a comma between independent word groups connected by *and, but, for, or, nor, so, yet* (as in "I already had it recharged once, so . . .").

1. • Louise used a dandruff shampoo.
   • She still had dandruff.
   • She decided to see a dermatologist.

   _____

   _____

   _____

2. • Omar's parents want him to be a doctor.
   • Omar wants to be a salesman.
   • He impresses people with his charm.

   _____

   _____

   _____

3. • The instructor conducted a discussion period.
   • Jack sat at his desk with his head down.
   • He did not want the instructor to call on him.
   • He had not read the assignment.

   _____

   _____

   _____

   _____

Do

Community Dialect		Standard English	
(Do not use in your writing)		**(Use for clear communication)**	

Present Tense

I does	we does	I do	we do
you does	you does	you do	you do
he, she, it do	they does	he, she, it does	they do

Past Tense

I done	we done	I did	we did
you done	you done	you did	you did
he, she, it done	they done	he, she, it did	they did

TIP   Many people have trouble with one negative form of *do*. They will say, for example, "She don't listen" instead of "She doesn't listen," or they will say "This pen don't work" instead of "This pen doesn't work." Be careful to avoid the common mistake of using *don't* instead of *doesn't*.

Underline the standard form of the irregular verb *be, have,* or *do.*

1. This week, my Aunt Charlotte (have, <u>has</u>) a dentist's appointment.

2. She (<u>does</u>, do) not enjoy going to the dentist.

3. She (<u>is</u>, are) always frightened by the shiny instruments.

4. The drills (is, <u>are</u>) the worst thing in the office.

5. When Aunt Charlotte (<u>was</u>, were) a little girl, she (have, had) a bad experience at the dentist's.

6. The dentist told her he (<u>was</u>, were) going to pull out all her teeth.

7. Aunt Charlotte (do, <u>did</u>) not realize that he (was, were) only joking.

8. Her parents (was, <u>were</u>) unprepared for her screams of terror.

9. Now, she (<u>has</u>, had) a bad attitude toward dentists.

10. She refuses to keep an appointment unless I (<u>am</u>, are) with her in the waiting room.

Practice

5

Practice 6

Cross out the nonstandard verb form in each sentence. Then write the standard form of *be, have,* or *do* in the space provided.

_is_   1. If it ~~be~~ not raining tomorrow, we're going camping.

are   2. You ~~is~~ invited to join us.

have   3. You ~~has~~ to bring your own sleeping bag and flashlight.

doesn't 4. It ~~don't~~ hurt to bring a raincoat also, in case of a sudden shower.

are   5. The stars ~~is~~ beautiful on a warm summer night.

had   6. Last year we ~~have~~ a great time on a family camping trip.

did   7. We ~~done~~ all the cooking ourselves.

had   8. The food tasted good even though it ~~have~~ some dead leaves in it.

had   9. Then we discovered that we ~~has~~ no insect repellent.

were   10. When we got home, we ~~was~~ covered with mosquito bites.

Practice 7

Fill in each blank with the standard form of *be, have,* or *do.*

My mother sings alto in our church choir. She _had_ to go to choir practice every Friday night and _was_ expected to know all the music. If she _did_ not know her part, the other choir members _did_ things like glare at her and _were_ likely to make nasty comments, she says. Last weekend, my mother _had_ houseguests and _did_ not have time to learn all the notes. The music _was_ very difficult, and she thought the other people _were_ going to make fun of her. But they _were_ very understanding when she told them that she _was_ laryngitis and couldn't make a sound.

Review Test 1

Underline the standard verb form.

1. Paul (pound, <u>pounded</u>) the mashed potatoes until they turned into glue.

2. The velvety banana (rest, <u>rests</u>) on the shiny counter.

3. My neighbor's daughter (have, <u>has</u>) a brand-new Toyota.

4. It (<u>is</u>, be) fire-engine red with black leather upholstery.

Draw one line under the subject. Then lightly cross out any words that come between the subject and the verb. Finally, draw two lines under the correct verb in parentheses.

EXAMPLE

The price ~~of the stereo speakers~~ (is, are) too high for my wallet.

1. The blue stain ~~on the sheets~~ (comes, come) from the cheap dish towel that I put in the washer with them.

2. The sport coat, ~~along with the two pairs of pants,~~ (sells, sell) for just fifty dollars.

3. The roots ~~of the apple tree~~ (is, are) very shallow.

4. Amir's sisters, ~~who wanted to be at his surprise party,~~ (was, were) unable to come because of flooded roads.

5. The dust-covered photo albums in the attic (belongs, belong) to my grandmother.

6. The cost of personal calls made on office telephones (is, are) deducted from our pay.

7. Two cups of coffee in the morning (does, do) not make up a hearty breakfast.

8. The moon as well as some stars (is, are) shining brightly tonight.

9. The electrical wiring in the apartment (is, are) dangerous and needs replacing.

10. Chapter 4 of the psychology book, along with six weeks of class notes, (is, are) to be the basis of the test.

Verb before the Subject

A verb agrees with its subject even when the verb comes *before* the subject. Words that may precede the subject include *there, here,* and, in questions, *who, which, what,* and *where.*

Inside the storage shed are the garden tools.

At the street corner were two panhandlers.

There are times I'm ready to quit my job.

Where are the instructions for the iPod?

> **TIP** If you are unsure about the subject, ask *who* or *what* of the verb. With the first sentence above, you might ask, "What are inside the storage shed?" The answer, garden *tools,* is the subject.

Practice

2

Underline the subject in each sentence. Then double-underline the correct verb in parentheses.

1. There (is, are) long lines at the checkout counter.

2. Scampering to the door to greet Martha Grencher (was, were) her two little dogs.

3. Filling the forest floor (was, were) dozens of pine cones.

4. There (is, are) pretzels if you want something to go with the cheese.

5. At the end of the line, hoping to get seats for the movie, (was, were) Janet and Maureen.

6. There (is, are) rats nesting under the backyard woodpile.

7. Swaggering down the street (was, were) several tough-looking boys.

8. On the very top of that mountain (is, are) a house for sale.

9. At the soap opera convention, there (was, were) fans from all over the country.

10. Under a large plastic dome on the side of the counter (lies, lie) a single gooey pastry.

Indefinite Pronouns

The following words, known as *indefinite pronouns,* always take singular verbs.

Indefinite Pronouns			
(-*one* words)	(-*body* words)	(-*thing* words)	
one	nobody	nothing	each
anyone	anybody	anything	either
everyone	everybody	everything	neither
someone	somebody	something	

TIP *Both* always takes a plural verb.

Write the correct form of the verb in the space provided.

hope, hopes 1. Everyone in our neighborhood _hopes_ the farm stays open.

dances, dance 2. Nobody _dances_ the way he does.

deserves, deserve 3. Either of our football team's guards _deserve_ to be an all-state guard.

was, were 4. Both of the race drivers _were_ injured.

appears, appear 5. Everyone who received an invitation _appears_ to be here.

offers, offer 6. No one ever _offers_ to work on that committee.

owns, own 7. One of my sisters _owns_ a VW convertible.

has, have 8. Somebody _____ been taking shopping carts from the supermarket.

thinks, think 9. Everyone that I talked to _____ the curfew is a good idea.

has, have 10. Each of the candidates _____ talked about withdrawing from the race.

Compound Subjects

Subjects joined by *and* generally take a plural verb.

> Yoga and biking are Lola's ways of staying in shape.

> Ambition and good luck are the keys to his success.

When subjects are joined by *or, either… or, neither… nor, not only… but also,* the verb agrees with the subject closer to the verb.

> Either the restaurant manager or his assistants deserve to be fired for the spoiled meat used in the stew.

The nearer subject, *assistants,* is plural, and so the verb is plural.

Write the correct form of the verb in the space provided.

matches, match 1. This tie and shirt _match_ the suit, but the shoes look terrible.

has, have 2. The kitchen and the bathroom _have_ to be cleaned.

is, are 3. A good starting salary and a bonus system _are_ the most attractive features of my new job.

plan, plans 4. Neither Ellen nor her brothers _____ to work at a temporary job during their holiday break from college.

is, are 5. For better or worse, working on his van and playing video games _____ Pete's main interests in life.

www.mhhe.com/langan

Who, Which, and That

When *who*, *which*, and *that* are used as subjects, they take singular verbs if the word they stand for is singular and plural verbs if the word they stand for is plural. For example, in the sentence

Gary is one of those people who are very private.

the verb is plural because *who* stands for *people*, which is plural. On the other hand, in the sentence

Gary is a person who is very private.

the verb is singular because *who* stands for *person*, which is singular.

Practice

5

Write the correct form of the verb in the space provided.

was, were

1. I removed the sheets that _were_ jamming my washer.

stumbles, stumble

2. This job isn't for people who _stumble_ over tough decisions.

blares, blare

3. The radio that _blares_ all night belongs to my insomniac neighbor.

gives, give

4. The Saturn is one of the small American cars that _give_ high gasoline mileage.

appears, appear

5. The strange smell that _appears_ in our neighborhood on rainy days is being investigated.

Collaborative Activity

Editing and Rewriting

Working with a partner, read the short paragraph below and mark off the five mistakes in subject-verb agreement. Then use the space provided to correct the five agreement errors. Feel free to discuss the rewrite quietly with your partner and refer back to the chapter when necessary.

When most people think about cities, they do not thinks about wild

animals. But in my city apartment, there is [are] enough creatures to fill a small

forest. In the daytime, I must contend with the pigeons. These unwanted

guests of my apartment makes a loud feathery mess on my bedroom

windowsill. In the evening, my apartment is visited by roaches. These

large insects creep onto my kitchen floor and walls after dark and frighten me with their shiny glistening bodies. Later at night, my apartment is invaded by mice. Waking from sleep, I can hear their little feet tapping as they scurry behind walls and above my ceiling. Everybody I know think I should move into a new apartment. What I really need is to go somewhere that have less wild creatures—maybe a forest!

Think   ~~t~~   ¦ are
Make   Has
Thinks

Collaborative Activity

Creating Sentences

Working with a partner, write sentences as directed. With each item, pay special attention to subject-verb agreement.

1. Write a sentence in which the words *in the cafeteria* or *on the table* come between the subject and verb. Underline the subject of your sentence and circle the verb.

2. Look at the photo and write a sentence that begins with the words *there is* or *there are*. Underline the subject of your sentence and circle the verb.

3. Write a sentence in which the indefinite pronoun *nobody* or *anything* is the subject.

4. Write a sentence with the compound subjects *manager* and *employees*. Underline the subject of your sentence and circle the verb.

Reflective Activity

1. Look at the paragraph about the apartment that you revised above. Which rule involving subject-verb agreement gave you the most trouble? How did you figure out the correct answer?

2. Explain which of the five subject-verb agreement situations discussed in this chapter is most likely to cause you problems.

Review Test   1

Complete each of the following sentences, using *is*, *are*, *was*, *were*, *have*, or *has*. Underline the subject of each of these verbs.

EXAMPLE

The <u>hot dogs</u> in that luncheonette *are hazardous to your health.*

1. Neither of the songs _____

   _____

2. The new state tax on alcohol and cigarettes _____

   _____

3. The shadowy figure behind the cemetery walls _____

   _____

4. The movie actress and her agent _____

   _____

5. Larry is one of those people who _____

   _____

6. The football coach, along with ten of his assistants, _____

   _____

7. The students in the computer lab _____

_____

8. Someone sitting in the left-field bleachers of the ballpark _____

_____

9. The first several weeks that I spent in college _____

_____

10. Tony's gentle voice and pleasant smile _____

_____

Review Test 2

Underline the correct word in the parentheses.

1. Excessive use of alcohol, caffeine, or cigarettes (damages, damage) a mother's unborn child.

2. Neither of the newspaper articles (gives, give) all the facts of the murder case.

3. There (is, are) five formulas that we have to memorize for the test.

4. The rug and the wallpaper in that room (has, have) to be replaced.

5. The old man standing under the park trees (does, do) not look happy.

6. The scratch on the record (was, were) there when I bought it.

7. Heavy snows and months of subfreezing temperatures (is, are) two reasons why I moved to Florida.

8. I don't enjoy people who (likes, like) to play pranks.

9. The price of the set of dishes you like so much (is, are) $345.

10. What time in the morning (does, do) planes leave for Denver?

Review Test 3

There are eight mistakes in subject-verb agreement in the following passage. Cross out each incorrect verb and write the correct form above it. In addition, underline the subject of each of the verbs that must be changed.

There are several things that makes Tracy want to quit her job as a waitress. First of all, she is never permitted to sit down. Even when there is no customers seated at her tables, she must find something useful to do, such as folding napkins or refilling ketchup bottles. By the end of the night, her feet feel like two chunks of raw hamburger. Second, she finds it difficult to be cheerful all of the time, but cheerfulness is one of the qualities that is expected of her. People who go out to eat in a restaurant wants to enjoy themselves, and they don't like their spirits dampened by a grouchy waitress. This means that when Tracy feels sick or depressed, she can't let her feelings show. Instead, she has to pretend that the occasion is as pleasant for her as it is for her customers, night after night. Neither of these problems, however, bother her as much as people who are fussy. Both the child who demands extra fudge sauce on her ice cream and the adult who asks for cleaner silverware has to be satisfied. In addition, each night at least one of the customers at her tables insist on being a perfectionist. As Tracy learned her first day on the job, the customer is always right—even if he complains that the peas have too many wrinkles. Though she may feel like dumping the peas into the customer's lap, Tracy must pretend that each of her customers are royalty and hurry to find some less wrinkled peas. Sometimes she wishes people would just stay home and eat.

Subject-Verb Agreement   MASTERY TEST 1

Underline the correct verb in the parentheses. Note that you will first have to
determine the subject in each sentence. To help find subjects in certain sentences,
you may find it helpful to cross out prepositional phrases.

1. The four flights of stairs up to my apartment (is, are) as steep as Mount
Everest sometimes.

2. The sweater and the books on the table (belongs, belong) to Keiko.

3. One of their sons (has, have) been expelled from school.

4. My brother and I (has, have) season tickets to the games.

5. Jake and Eva (enjoys, enjoy) watching old movies on television.

6. Either of the television sets (gives, give) excellent picture quality.

7. There (is, are) about ten things I must get done today.

8. Hurrying down the street after their father (was, were) two small children.

9. Here (is, are) the screwdriver you were looking for all weekend.

10. No one in this world (is, are) going to get out alive.

11. The plywood under your carpets (is, are) rotting.

12. Sex and violence (is, are) the mainstays of many popular movies.

13. Tamara and her sister Teresa (goes, go) to the gym to work out three times
per week.

14. Not only the manager but also the owners of the ball club (is, are)
responsible for the poor performance of the team.

15. There (is, are) a great deal of work yet to be done.

16. One of the women on the bowling team (has, have) won a million dollars in
the state lottery.

17. The study of statistics (is, are) important for a psychology major.

18. My father is a person who (cares, care) more about time with his family than
about success in his job.

19. The carpenter and the electrician (is, are) working at the house today.

20. I tug and pull, but the line of supermarket carts (seems, seem) welded together.

NAME: _____

DATE: _____

MASTERY TEST 2 Subject-Verb Agreement

In the space provided, write the correct form of the verb shown in the margin.

is, are
1. The chain-link fence surrounding the school grounds _____ ready to collapse.

plays, play
2. I envy people who _____ a musical instrument well.

is, are
3. Inside the bakery shop carton _____ your favorite pastries.

has, have
4. Someone on the team _____ forgotten her warm-up jacket.

wants, want
5. Because I spilled a beaker of sulfuric acid, nobody in my chemistry lab _____ to work with me.

is, are
6. At the end of the long movie line _____ about twenty people who will not get into the next show.

looks, look
7. Neither of the coats _____ good on you.

is, are
8. A little time for rest and relaxation _____ what I need right now.

was, were
9. The shirts that she thought _____ too expensive are now on sale.

shops, shop
10. Raquel and her mother _____ together on Thursday nights.

NAME: _____

DATE: _____

Subject-Verb Agreement MASTERY TEST 3

Cross out the incorrect form of the verb. In addition, underline the subject
that goes with the verb. Then write the correct form of the verb in the space
provided. Mark the one sentence that is correct with a *C*.

_____ 1. The price of the computer games have been reduced.

_____ 2. The marigolds that was planted yesterday were accidentally mowed over today.

_____ 3. Many tables at the auction was covered with very old books.

_____ 4. Brenda checked with the employment agencies that was helping her look for a job.

_____ 5. Trucks and cars uses our street heavily since road construction began.

_____ 6. The old woman rooting through those trash baskets have refused to enter a nursing home.

_____ 7. The vicious gossip about our new neighbor have begun to anger me.

_____ 8. Donovan plays two sports and are good at both of them.

_____ 9. The plastic slipcovers on their furniture has started to turn yellow.

_____ 10. Either my willpower or my lust for chocolate has to win out.

NAME: _____

DATE: _____

MASTERY TEST 4 | Subject-Verb Agreement

Cross out the incorrect form of the verb. In addition, underline the subject that goes with the verb. Then write the correct form of the verb in the space provided. Mark the one sentence that is correct with a *C*.

_____ 1. Why has Cindy and Karen quit their jobs as telephone repair persons?

_____ 2. One actress at the rehearsals have become ill from the heat.

_____ 3. The buildings across the street is all going to be demolished.

_____ 4. Those old coats in your closet has dust lying on their shoulders.

_____ 5. Archery and soccer is the new sports at our school.

_____ 6. If only there was more hours in the day, I could get all my work done.

_____ 7. Two pieces of dry toast and a soft-boiled egg is all Rita is allowed to eat for breakfast.

_____ 8. One of the waitresses at the diner have just won a free trip to Las Vegas.

_____ 9. Lola's long red silk scarf and her lipstick match perfectly.

_____ 10. Anything that parents tell their children usually get ignored.

DATE: _____

Subject-Verb Agreement **MASTERY TEST 5**

Underline the correct verb in the parentheses. Note that you will first have
to determine the subject in each sentence. To help find subjects in certain
sentences, you may find it helpful to cross out prepositional phrases.

1. All the animals for sale in that pet store (looks, look) unhealthy.

2. The extra fees on my new cell phone bill (is, are) too high.

3. One of my instructors (has, have) a hybrid car.

4. Wet roads and dangerous driving (was, were) to blame for the accident.

5. Not one cash register in the store (is, are) working correctly.

6. Once a year, Jim and his buddies (goes, go) fishing.

7. The books in the library (was, were) damaged by the flood.

8. Crawling across the kitchen floor (was, were) three hairy spiders.

9. The employees of the hospital (wants, want) a pay raise.

10. Neither Kevin nor Denise (wants, want) to talk about their relationship.

11. A stack of folded shirts in the Laundromat (was, were) stolen.

12. Someone once said, "Politics (is, are) a dirty business."

13. A few kids on the high school team (hopes, hope) to play college football.

14. Hakeem is one of those guys who (knows, know) how to fix anything.

15. The buttons on the old keyboard (is, are) dirty from use.

16. The executives of that company (makes, make) ten times as much as any of
their employees.

17. The old houses across the street on our block (needs, need) major repairs.

18. Shoppers in the long line at the closeout sale in the mall (was, were)
muttering angrily to themselves.

19. Physics (is, are) a subject that requires strong math skills.

20. The chrome wheels on the classic Ford Mustang (shines, shine).

Consistent Verb Tense

Introductory Activity

See if you can find and underline the two mistakes in verb tense in the following selection.

When Computer Warehouse had a sale, Alex decided to buy a new personal computer. He planned to set up the machine himself and hoped to connect it to the Internet right away. When he arrived home, however, Alex discovers that hooking up the wires to the computer could be complicated and confusing. The directions sounded as if they had been written for electrical engineers. After two hours of frustration, Alex gave up and calls a technician for help.

Now try to complete the following statement:

Verb tenses should be consistent. In the selection above, two verbs have to be changed because they are mistakenly in the (*present, past*) _____ tense while all the other verbs in the selection are in the (*present, past*) _____ tense.

Answers are on page 564.

Keeping Tenses Consistent

Do not shift tenses unnecessarily. If you begin writing a paper in the present tense, don't shift suddenly to the past. If you begin in the past, don't shift without reason to the present. Notice the inconsistent verb tenses in the following example:

> Smoke <u>spilled</u> from the front of the overheated car. The driver <u>opens</u> up the hood, then <u>jumped</u> back as steam <u>billows</u> out.

The verbs must be consistently in the present tense:

> Smoke <u>spills</u> from the front of the overheated car. The driver <u>opens</u> up the hood, then <u>jumps</u> back as steam <u>billows</u> out.

Or the verbs must be consistently in the past tense:

> Smoke <u>spilled</u> from the front of the overheated car. The driver <u>opened</u> up the hood, then <u>jumped</u> back as steam <u>billowed</u> out.

www.mhhe.com/langan

In each item, one verb must be changed so that it agrees in tense with the other verbs. Cross out the incorrect verb and write the correct form in the space at the left.

Practice

1

EXAMPLE

looked   I gave away my striped sweater after three people told me I ~~look~~ like a giant bee.

_____ 1. Mike peels and eats oranges at movies; the smell caused other people to move away from him.

_____ 2. The nursing program attracted Juanita, but she weighed the pluses and minuses and then decides to enroll in the x-ray technician course instead.

_____ 3. I grabbed for the last bag of pretzels on the supermarket shelf. But when I pick it up, I discovered there was a tear in the cellophane bag.

_____ 4. Roger waits eagerly for the mail carrier each day. Part of him hoped to get a letter in which someone declares she is madly in love with him and will cherish him forever.

_____ 5. The first thing Jerry does every day is weigh himself. The scale informed him what he can eat that day.

_____ 6. My sister sprinkles detergent flakes on my head and then ran around telling everyone that I had dandruff.

_____ 7. When Norm peeled back the old shingles, he discovers that the roof was rotted through.

NAME: _____

DATE: _____

MASTERY TEST 1 | Consistent Verb Tense

In each item, one verb must be changed so that it agrees in tense with the other verbs. Cross out the inconsistent verb and write the correct form in the space provided.

_____ 1. After my brother downloads all his music onto his new iPod, he wound up listening to his old records on the turntable he found in our attic.

_____ 2. The little boy raced his Lionel train too fast, so that it topples off the track when it rounded a curve.

_____ 3. She let her mother cut her hair until her friends began saying that her hairstyle looks very strange.

_____ 4. The air pollution is so bad that the weather bureau urges people not to exercise outside until it cleared.

_____ 5. Tarik scrolls through his hundreds of new emails; he hoped to find one from his new girlfriend.

_____ 6. After the truck overturned, passing motorists parked their cars on the side of the road and walk back to look at the damage.

_____ 7. The lights went out and we all jump because we were watching a horror movie at the time.

_____ 8. The wind came up quickly, knocks down a lot of dead tree branches, and blew in the front window of the bank across the street.

_____ 9. After the wolf unsuccessfully huffed and puffed at the little pigs' brick house, he realizes he would have to hire a demolition contractor.

_____ 10. While in the hospital, she read lots of magazines, watched daytime television, shuffles up and down the corridor, and generally felt very bored.

NAME: _____

DATE: _____

Consistent Verb Tense MASTERY TEST 2

In each item, one verb must be changed so that it agrees in tense with the other verb or verbs. Cross out the inconsistent verb and write the correct form in the space provided.

_____ 1. Irina likes to search for old high school friends on Facebook, but she never seemed to find them.

_____ 2. Tony reached way down into the bread bag. He skipped the first couple of pieces and grabs one of the fresher, bigger pieces from the middle.

_____ 3. Darrell believes he is smarter than we are; he tried to show this all the time.

_____ 4. When I noticed the way my mother cocked her head, I realize that she had an earache.

_____ 5. When we asked for a fresh tablecloth, the waiter looks as though we were speaking Russian.

_____ 6. As the tourists walked through the forest, they cheek the trail markers that were posted along the way.

_____ 7. My eyes always close and my fingers get numb when I listened to an afternoon lecture in Professor Snorrel's class.

_____ 8. Leon graduated from Camden High School, works as a plumber's assistant for two years, and then returned to school.

_____ 9. At holiday dinners, many people continue to stuff themselves even when it seemed obvious that they are already full.

_____ 10. I wiped my hands on my trousers before I walk in for the job interview. I did not want the personnel officer to know my palms were sweating.

Additional Information about Verbs

12

The purpose of this special chapter is to provide additional information about verbs. Some people will find the grammatical terms here a helpful reminder of earlier school learning about verbs. For them, these terms will increase their understanding of how verbs function in English. Other people may welcome more detailed information about terms used elsewhere in the text. In either case, remember that the most common mistakes people make when using verbs have been treated in earlier sections of the book.

Verb Tense

Verbs tell us the time of an action. The time that a verb shows is usually called *tense*. The most common tenses are the simple present, past, and future. In addition, there are nine other tenses that enable us to express more specific ideas about time than we could with the simple tenses alone. In the box on the facing page are the twelve verb tenses, and examples of each tense. Read them to increase your sense of the many different ways of expressing time in English.

Tenses	Examples
Present	I *work*. Tanya *works*.
Past	Howard *worked* on the lawn.
Future	You *will work* overtime this week.
Present perfect	Gail *has worked* hard on the puzzle. They *have worked* well together.
Past perfect	They *had worked* eight hours before their shift ended.
Future perfect	The volunteers *will have worked* many unpaid hours.
Present progressive	I *am* not *working* today. You *are working* the second shift. The clothes dryer *is* not *working* properly.
Past progressive	She *was working* outside. The plumbers *were working* here this morning.
Future progressive	The sound system *will be working* by tonight.
Present perfect progressive	Married life *has* not *been working* out for that couple.
Past perfect progressive	I *had been working* overtime until recently.
Future perfect progressive	My sister *will have been working* at that store for eleven straight months by the time she takes a vacation next week.

www.mhhe.com/langan

The perfect tenses are formed by adding *have, has,* or *had* to the past participle (the form of the verb that ends, usually, in *-ed*). The progressive tenses are formed by adding *am, is, are, was,* or *were* to the present participle (the form of the verb that ends in *-ing*). The perfect progressive tenses are formed by adding *have been, has been,* or *had been* to the present participle.

Certain tenses are explained in more detail on the following pages.

Present Perfect
(*have* or *has* + past participle)

The present perfect tense expresses an action that began in the past and has recently been completed or is continuing in the present.

> The city *has* just *agreed* on a contract with the sanitation workers.
>
> Tony's parents *have lived* in that house for twenty years.
>
> Sarah *has enjoyed* vampire novels since she was a little girl.

Past Perfect
(*had* + past participle)

The past perfect tense expresses a past action that was completed before another past action.

> Lola *had learned* to dance by the time she was five.
>
> The class *had* just *started* when the fire bell rang.
>
> Bad weather *had* never *been* a problem on our vacations until last year.

Present Progressive
(*am, is,* or *are* + *-ing* form)

The present progressive tense expresses an action still in progress.

> I *am taking* an early train into the city every day this week.
>
> Karl *is playing* softball over at the field.
>
> The vegetables *are growing* rapidly.

Past Progressive
(*was* or *were* + *-ing* form)

The past progressive expresses an action that was in progress in the past.

> I *was spending* several hours a day following celebrities on Twitter before I got bored and started writing songs.
>
> Last week, the store *was selling* many items at half price.
>
> My friends *were driving* over to pick me up when the accident occurred.

Practice

1

For the sentences that follow, fill in the present or past perfect or the present or past progressive of the verb shown. Use the tense that seems to express the meaning of each sentence best.

Additional Information about Verbs MASTERY TEST 1

PART A

In each space, write the **present perfect tense** form of the verb shown.

practice

1. Carlos _____ his speech each night for the past week.

search

2. Divers _____ the sunken ship looking for lost treasure.

clean

3. As of today, volunteers _____ three vacant lots for the new neighborhood garden.

PART B

In each space, write the **past perfect tense** form of the verb shown.

hike

4. Ray _____ for an hour when he noticed a bear following him.

inspect

5. My father _____ the old car twice before he agreed to buy it.

PART C

In each space, write the **present progressive tense** form of the verb shown.

sing

6. Our neighbors _____ in the church choir tonight.

run

7. Sandra _____ in the New York City marathon.

PART D

In each space, write the **past progressive tense** form of the verb shown.

talk

8. Last night, Jessica _____ for hours on the phone.

plan

9. Until he was severely injured in a car bombing, the soldier _____ to get married this summer.

eat

10. Before he started his diet, Phil _____ ice cream after each meal.

NAME: _____

DATE: _____

MASTERY TEST 2

Additional Information about Verbs

PART 1

In the space provided, identify the italicized word as a participle (*P*), an infinitive (*I*), or a gerund (*G*).

_____ 1. The *blaring* siren woke up the entire neighborhood.

_____ 2. *Cooking* helps Mimi relax when she is stressed.

_____ 3. After school, the boys wanted *to play* chess.

_____ 4. Too much *drinking* ruined Paul's first semester of college.

_____ 5. *Crumbling* walls are all that remains of the homes in the abandoned neighborhood.

PART 2

Change the following sentences from the passive to the active voice. Note that you may have to add a subject in some cases.

1. The wooden floor in our living room was eaten by termites.

   _____

2. A small bonus was given to each employee by the store manager.

   _____

3. Food and shelter were donated to the survivors of the storm.

   _____

4. Tomatoes and peppers were planted in the backyard by Maria.

   _____

5. A threat to bomb the high school was made by an angry student.

   _____

Pronoun Reference, Agreement, and Point of View

Introductory Activity

Read each pair of sentences below, noting the underlined pronouns. Then see if you can circle the correct letter in each of the statements that follow.

1. a. Only one of the nominees for "best actress" showed their anxiety as the names were being read.

   b. Only one of the nominees for "best actress" showed her anxiety as the names were being read.

2. a. At the mall, they are already putting up Christmas decorations.

   b. At the mall, shop owners are already putting up Christmas decorations.

3. a. I go to the steak house often because you can get inexpensive meals there.

   b. I go to the steak house often because I can get inexpensive meals there.

In the first pair, (a, b) uses the underlined pronoun correctly because the pronoun refers to *one*, which is a singular word.

In the second pair, (a, b) is correct because otherwise the pronoun reference would be unclear.

In the third pair, (a, b) is correct because the pronoun point of view should not be shifted unnecessarily.

Answers are on page 564.

Pronouns are words that take the place of nouns (words for persons, places, or things). In fact, the word *pronoun* means *for a noun*. Pronouns are shortcuts that keep you from unnecessarily repeating words in writing. Here are some examples of pronouns:

Martha shampooed *her* dog. (*Her* is a pronoun that takes the place of *Martha's*.)

As the door swung open, *it* creaked. (*It* replaces *door*.)

When the motorcyclists arrived at McDonald's, *they* removed *their* helmets. (*They* replaces *motorcyclists; their* replaces *motorcyclists'*.)

This chapter presents rules that will help you avoid three common mistakes people make with pronouns. The rules are as follows:

1. A pronoun must refer clearly to the word it replaces.
2. A pronoun must agree in number with the word or words it replaces.
3. Pronouns should not shift unnecessarily in point of view.

www.mhhe.com/langan

Pronoun Reference

A sentence may be confusing and unclear if a pronoun appears to refer to more than one word, as in this sentence:

I locked my suitcase in my car, and then it was stolen.

What was stolen? It is unclear whether the suitcase or the car was stolen.

I locked my suitcase in my car, and then my car was stolen.

A sentence may also be confusing if the pronoun does not refer to any specific word. Look at this sentence:

We never buy fresh vegetables at that store because they charge too much.

Who charges too much? There is no specific word that *they* refers to. Be clear.

We never buy fresh vegetables at that store because the owners charge too much.

Here are additional sentences with unclear pronoun reference. Read the explanations of why they are unclear and look carefully at the ways they are corrected.

Points to Remember about Relative Pronouns

Point 1

Whose means *belonging to whom.* Be careful not to confuse *whose* with *who's,* which means *who is.*

Point 2

Who, whose, and *whom* all refer to people. *Which* refers to things. *That* can refer to either people or things.

> I don't know *whose* book this is.
>
> Don't sit on the chair, *which* is broken.
>
> Let's elect a captain *that* cares about winning.

Point 3

Who, whose, whom, and *which* can also be used to ask questions. When they are used in this way, they are called *interrogative* pronouns:

> *Who* murdered the secret agent?
>
> *Whose* fingerprints were on the bloodstained knife?
>
> To *whom* have the detectives been talking?
>
> *Which* suspect is going to confess?

TIP In informal usage, *who* is generally used instead of *whom* as an interrogative pronoun. Informally, we can say or write, "*Who* are you rooting for in the game?" or "*Who* did the instructor fail?" More formal usage would use *whom:* "Whom are you rooting for in the game?" and "Whom did the instructor fail?"

Point 4

Who and *whom* are used differently. *Who* is a subject pronoun. Use *who* as the subject of a verb:

> Let's see *who* will be teaching the course.

Whom is an object pronoun. Use *whom* as the object of a verb or a preposition:

> Dr. Kelsey is the instructor *whom* I like best.
>
> I haven't decided for *whom* I will vote.

You may want to review the material on subject and object pronouns on pages 217–220.

Here is an easy way to decide whether to use *who* or *whom*. Find the first verb after the place where the *who* or *whom* will go. See if it already has a subject. If it does have a subject, use the object pronoun *whom*. If there is no subject, give it one by using the subject pronoun *who*. Notice how *who* and *whom* are used in the sentences that follow:

> I don't know *who* sideswiped my car.

> The suspect *whom* the police arrested finally confessed.

In the first sentence, *who* is used to give the verb *sideswiped* a subject. In the second sentence, the verb *arrested* already has a subject, *police*. Therefore, *whom* is the correct pronoun.

Practice

3

Underline the correct pronoun in each of the following sentences.

1. My grandfather, (who, which) is seventy-nine, goes bowling every Friday.

2. The plant (who, that) Nita got for her birthday finally died.

3. I wish I had a relative (who, whom) would give me a million dollars.

4. I don't know to (who, whom) I should send my complaint letter.

5. Nobody knew (who, whom) was responsible for the mistake.

Practice

4

On separate paper, write five sentences using *who, whose, whom, which,* and *that.*

Possessive Pronouns

Possessive pronouns show ownership or possession.

> Clyde shut off the engine of *his* motorcycle.

> The keys are *mine*.

Here is a list of possessive pronouns:

Possessive Pronouns	
my, mine	our, ours
your, yours	your, yours
his	their, theirs
her, hers	
its	

Adjectives and Adverbs

Introductory Activity

Write in an appropriate word or words to complete each of the sentences below.

1. The teenage years were a _____ time for me.
2. The mechanic listened _____ while I described my car problem.
3. Basketball is a _____ game than football.
4. My brother is the _____ person in our family.

Now see if you can complete the following sentences.

The word inserted in the first sentence is an (adjective, adverb); it describes the word *time*.

The word inserted in the second sentence is an (adjective, adverb); it probably ends in the two letters _____ and describes the word *listened*.

The word inserted in the third sentence is a comparative adjective; it may be preceded by *more* or end in the two letters _____.

The word inserted in the fourth sentence is a superlative adjective; it may be preceded by *most* or end in the three letters _____.

Answers are on page 566.

Adjectives and adverbs are descriptive words. Their purpose is to make the meaning of the words they describe more specific.

www.mhhe.com/langan

Adjectives

What Are Adjectives?

Adjectives describe nouns (names of persons, places, or things) or pronouns.

> Charlotte is a *kind* woman. (The adjective *kind* describes the noun *woman*.)
>
> He is *tired*. (The adjective *tired* describes the pronoun *he*.)

An adjective usually comes before the word it describes (as in *kind woman*). But it can also come after forms of the verb *be* (*is, are, was, were*, and so on). Less often, an adjective follows verbs such as *feel, look, smell, sound, taste, appear, become*, and *seem*.

> The bureau is *heavy*. (The adjective *heavy* describes the bureau.)
>
> These pants are *itchy*. (The adjective *itchy* describes the pants.)
>
> The children seem *restless*. (The adjective *restless* describes the children.)

What is your opinion of the above artwork? What thoughts and feelings come to mind as you view it? On a separate piece of paper, use adjectives to describe your feelings about this artwork. Write at least three sentences using adjectives.

Using Adjectives to Compare

For most short adjectives, add *-er* when comparing two things and *-est* when comparing three or more things.

I am *taller* than my brother, but my father is the *tallest* person in the house.

The farm market sells *fresher* vegetables than the corner store, but the *freshest* vegetables are the ones grown in my own garden.

For most *longer* adjectives (two or more syllables), add *more* when comparing two things and *most* when comparing three or more things.

Backgammon is *more enjoyable* to me than checkers, but chess is the *most enjoyable* game of all.

My mother is *more talkative* than my father, but my grandfather is the *most talkative* person in the house.

Points to Remember about Adjectives

Point 1

Be careful not to use both an *-er* ending and *more*, or both an *-est* ending and *most*.

Incorrect	Correct
Football is a *more livelier* game than baseball.	Football is a *livelier* game than baseball.
Tod Traynor was voted the *most likeliest* to succeed in our high school class.	Tod Traynor was voted the *most likely* to succeed in our high school class.

Point 2

Pay special attention to the following words, each of which has irregular forms.

	Comparative (Two)	Superlative (Three or More)
bad	worse	worst
good, well	better	best
little	less	least
much, many	more	most

Practice

1

Fill in the comparative or superlative forms for the following adjectives. Two are done for you as examples.

	Comparative (Two)	Superlative (Three or More)
fast	*faster*	*fastest*
timid	*more timid*	*most timid*
kind		
ambitious		
generous		
fine		
likable		

Practice

2

Add to each sentence the correct form of the word in the margin.

EXAMPLE

bad   The _____*worst*_____ day of my life was the one when my

house caught fire.

comfortable   1. My jeans are the _____ pants I own.

difficult   2. My biology exam was the _____ of my five exams.

easy   3. The _____ way to get a good grade in the class is

to take effective notes.

little   4. I made _____ money in my job as a delivery boy

than I made as a golf caddy.

good   5. The _____ pay I ever made was as a drill press

operator in a machine shop.

long   6. The ticket lines for the rock concert were the _____

I had ever seen.

memorable   7. The _____ days of my childhood were the ones I

spent on trips with my grandfather.

experienced   8. I am a _____ driver than my sister, but my

brother is the _____ driver in the family.

Collaborative Activity

Creating Sentences

Working with a partner, make up your own short test on faulty parallelism, as directed.

1. Write a sentence that includes three things you want to do tomorrow. One of those things should not be in parallel form. Then correct the faulty parallelism.

   Nonparallel _____

   _____

   Parellel _____

   _____

2. Write a sentence that names three positive qualities of a person you like or three negative qualities of a person you don't like.

   Nonparallel _____

   _____

   Parellel _____

   _____

3. Write a sentence that includes three everyday things that annoy you.

   Nonparallel _____

   _____

   Parellel _____

   _____

Reflective Activity

1. Look at the paragraph on defense mechanisms that you revised above. How has the attention to parallel form improved the paragraph?

2. How would you evaluate your use of parallel form in your writing? Do you use it almost never, at times, or often? How would you benefit from using it more?

Review Test 1

Cross out the unbalanced part of each sentence. Then rewrite the unbalanced part so that it matches the other item or items in the sentence.

EXAMPLE

I enjoy watering the grass and ~~to work~~ in the garden.

working
_____

1. Our production supervisor warned Jed to punch in on time, dress appropriately for the job, and he should stop taking extra breaks.

_____

2. On his ninetieth birthday, the old man mused that his long life was due to hard work, a loving wife, and because he had a sense of humor.

_____

3. The philosopher's advice is to live for the present, find some joy in each day, and by helping others.

_____

4. Freshly prepared food, an attractive decor, and having prompt service are signs of a good restaurant.

_____

5. Tarah has tickets for reckless driving, speeding, and she parked illegally.

_____

6. Washing clothes, cooking meals, and to take care of children used to be called "women's work."

_____

7. Our compact car provides better mileage; more comfort is provided by our station wagon.

_____

8. As the first bartender to arrive each day, Elena must slice lemons, get ice, and she has to check the inventory.

_____

Sentence Variety II

19

Like Chapter 7, this chapter will show you several ways to write effective and varied sentences. You will increase your sense of the many ways available to you for expressing your ideas. The practices here will also reinforce much of what you have learned in this section about modifiers and the use of parallelism.

-ing Word Groups

Use an *-ing* word group at some point in a sentence. Here are examples:

> The doctor, *hoping* for the best, examined the X-rays.
>
> *Jogging* every day, I soon raised my energy level.

More information about *-ing* words, also known as *present participles,* appears on page 196.

Combine each pair of sentences below into one sentence by using an *-ing* word and omitting repeated words. Use a comma or commas to set off the *-ing* word group from the rest of the sentence.

Practice

1

EXAMPLE

- The diesel truck chugged up the hill.
- It spewed out smoke.

    Spewing out smoke, the diesel truck chugged up the hill.

or *The diesel truck, spewing out smoke, chugged up the hill.*

1. • Ginger refused to get out of bed.
   • She pulled the blue blanket over her head.

   _____

   _____

2. • Dad is able to forget the troubles of the day.
   • He putters around in his basement workshop.

   _____

   _____

3. • The crowd of dancers moved as one.
   • They swayed to the music.

   _____

   _____

4. • George tried to protect himself from the dampness of the room.
   • He wrapped a scarf around his neck.

   _____

   _____

5. • The woman listened intently to the earnest young man.
   • She caressed her hair.

   _____

   _____

Practice

2

On separate paper, write five sentences of your own that contain *-ing* word groups.

-ed Word Groups

Use an *-ed* word group at some point in a sentence. Here are examples:

Tired of studying, I took a short break.

Mary, *amused* by the joke, told it to a friend.

I opened my eyes wide, *shocked* by the red "F" on my paper.

More information about *-ed* words, also known as *past participles,* appears on page 196.

Combine each of the following pairs of sentences into one sentence by using an *-ed* word and omitting repeated words. Use a comma or commas to set off the *-ed* word group from the rest of the sentence.

Practice

3

EXAMPLE

- Tim woke up with a start.
- He was troubled by a dream.

  Troubled by a dream, Tim woke up with a start.

or *Tim, troubled by a dream, woke up with a start.*

1. • I called an exterminator.
   • I was bothered by roaches.

   _____

   _____

2. • Sam grew silent.
   • He was baffled by what had happened.

   _____

   _____

3. • The crowd began to file slowly out of the stadium.
   • They were stunned by the last-minute touchdown.

   _____

   _____

4. • I tried to stifle my grin.
   • I was amused but reluctant to show how I felt.

   _____

   _____

5. • Cindy lay on the couch.
   • She was exhausted from working all day.

   _____

   _____

On separate paper, write five sentences of your own that contain *-ed* word groups.

Practice

4

-ly Openers

Use an *-ly* word to open a sentence. Here are examples:

Gently, he mixed the chemicals together.

Anxiously, the contestant looked at the game clock.

Skillfully, the quarterback rifled a pass to his receiver.

More information about *-ly* words, which are also known as *adverbs,* appears on page 235.

Practice

5

Combine each of the following pairs of sentences into one sentence by starting with an *-ly* word and omitting repeated words. Place a comma after the opening *-ly* word.

EXAMPLE

- I gave several yanks to the starting cord of the lawn mower.
- I was angry.

  Angrily, I gave several yanks to the starting cord of the lawn mower.

1. • The burglars carried the flat-screen TV out of the house.
   • They were quiet.

   _____

   _____

2. • Janelle squirmed in her seat as she waited for her turn to speak.
   • She was nervous.

   _____

   _____

3. • I reinforced all the coat buttons with strong thread.
   • I was patient.

   _____

   _____

In four of the five following sentences, the writer has mistakenly used the title to help explain the first sentence. But as has already been stated, you must *not* rely on the title to help explain your first sentence.

Rewrite the sentences so that they stand independent of the title. Write *Correct* under the one sentence that is independent of the title.

EXAMPLE

Title: Flunking an Exam

First sentence: I managed to do this because of several bad habits.

Rewritten: *I managed to flunk an exam because of several bad habits.*

_____

1. Title: The Worst Day of My Life

    First sentence: It began when my supervisor at work gave me a message to call home.

    Rewritten: _____

    _____

2. Title: Catholic Church Services

    First sentence: They have undergone many changes in the last few decades.

    Rewritten: _____

    _____

3. Title: An Embarrassing Incident

    First sentence: This happened to me when I was working as a waitress at the Stanton Hotel.

    Rewritten: _____

    _____

4. Title: The Inability to Share

    First sentence: The inability to share can cause great strains in a relationship.

    Rewritten: _____

    _____

5. Title: Offensive Television Commercials

    First sentence: Many that I watch are degrading to human dignity.

    Rewritten: _____

    _____

Review Test

Use the space provided below to rewrite the following sentences from a student paper, correcting the mistakes in format.

	"my nursing home friends"
	I now count some of them among my good friends. I fi-
	rst went there just to keep a relative of mine company.
	That is when I learned some of them rarely got any visitors.
	Many were starved for conversation and friendship.
	At the time, I did not want to get involved. But what I

NAME: _____

DATE: _____

Paper Format MASTERY TEST 1

Identify the five mistakes in paper format in the student paper that follows. From the box below, choose the letters that describe the five mistakes and write those letters in the spaces provided in the order in which they appear in the paper.

> a. The title should not be underlined.
> b. The title should not be set off in quotation marks.
> c. There should not be a period at the end of a title.
> d. All the major words in a title should be capitalized.
> e. The title should just be several words and not a complete sentence.
> f. The first sentence of a paper should stand independent of the title.
> g. A line should be skipped between the title and the first line of the paper.
> h. The first line of a paper should be indented.
> i. The right-hand margin should not be crowded.
> j. Hyphenation should occur only between syllables.

	"Nervous times"
	There are three different times that I feel nervous. First of all, if
	I'm in a classroom full of students I don't know and I'm asked to
	answer a question, I may begin to stutter. Or I may know the
	answer, but my mind will just block out. Second, if I'm going out
	on a date with a guy for the first time, I won't eat. Eating when
	I'm nervous makes my fork tremble, and I'm likely to drop food on
	my clothes. Finally if I'm going to a job interview, I will practice
	at home what I'm going to say. But as soon as I'm alone with the
	interviewer, and he asks me if there's anything I'd like to say, I
	say something dumb like "I'm a people person, you know." One day
	I hope to overcome my nervousness.

1. _____ 2. _____ 3. _____ 4. _____ 5. _____

NAME: _____

DATE: _____

MASTERY TEST 2 | Paper Format

Identify the five mistakes in paper format in the student paper that follows. From the box below, choose the letters that describe the five mistakes and write those letters in the spaces provided in the order in which they appear in the paper.

---

a. The title should not be underlined.

b. The title should not be set off in quotation marks.

c. There should not be a period at the end of a title.

d. All the major words in a title should be capitalized.

e. The title should just be several words and not a complete sentence.

f. The first sentence of a paper should stand independent of the title.

g. A line should be skipped between the title and the first line of the paper.

h. The first line of a paper should be indented.

i. The right-hand margin should not be crowded.

j. Hyphenation should occur only between syllables.

---

	coming down with the flu
	I could tell that I was coming down with it. For one th-
	ing, my nose and throat were shutting down. I could not breathe
	through my nose at all, while my nose was running nonstop, so
	that I soon went through a box of tissues. My throat was sore,
	and when I was brave enough to speak, my voice sounded horrible.
	Another reason I knew I had the flu was fever and chills. The
	thermometer registered 102 degrees. My chills were so bad that
	to get warm I had to put on sweat socks, flannel pajamas, and a
	heavy robe, and I then had to get under two blankets and a
	sheet. Finally, I was extremely fatigued. After I got into bed, I
	slept for eight hours straight. When I woke up I was still so tired
	that I couldn't get out of bed. My eyelids felt as if they weighed
	a hundred pounds each, and I could not lift my head off the pillow.
	Too tired to think, I drifted back to sleep with hazy thoughts of
	my mother's homemade chicken soup.

1. _____   2. _____   3. _____   4. _____   5. _____

Capital Letters

Introductory Activity

You probably already know a good deal about the uses of capital letters. Answering the questions below will help you check your knowledge before you begin the chapter.

1. Write the full name of a good friend: _____

2. In what city and state were you born? _____

3. What is your present street address? _____

4. Name a country where you would like to travel: _____

5. Name a school that you attended: _____

6. Give the name of a store where you buy food: _____

7. Name a company where you or anyone you know works:

   _____

8. Which day of the week gives you the best chance to relax? _____

9. What holiday is your favorite? _____

10. Which brand of toothpaste do you use? _____

11. Give the brand name of candy or chewing gum you like: _____

12. Name a song or a television show you enjoy: _____

13. Write the title of a magazine or newspaper you read:

    _____

continued

Three capital letters are needed in the example below. Underline the words you think should be capitalized. Then write them, capitalized, in the spaces provided.

on a beautiful, clear night last September, my roommate said, "let's buy some snacks and invite a few friends over to watch the meteor shower up on the roof." i knew my plans to get started on my term paper would have to be changed.

14. _____   15. _____   16. _____

Answers are on page 569.

Main Uses of Capital Letters

www.mhhe.com/langan

Capital letters are used with:

1. The first word in a sentence or direct quotation
2. Names of persons and the word *I*
3. Names of particular places
4. Names of days of the week, months, and holidays
5. Names of commercial products
6. Titles of books, magazines, articles, films, television shows, songs, poems, stories, papers that you write, and the like
7. Names of companies, associations, unions, clubs, religious and political groups, and other organizations

Each use is illustrated on the pages that follow.

First Word in a Sentence or Direct Quotation

Our company has begun laying people off.

The doctor said, "This may hurt a bit."

"My husband," said Sheryl, "is a light eater. When it's light, he starts to eat."

In the third example above, *My* and *When* are capitalized because they start new sentences. But *is* is not capitalized, because it is part of the first sentence.

Names of Persons and the Word *I*

At the picnic, I met Tony Curry and Lola Morrison.

Names of Particular Places

After graduating from Gibbs High School in Houston, I worked for a summer at a nearby Holiday Inn on Clairmont Boulevard.

But Use small letters if the specific name of a place is not given.

After graduating from high school in my hometown, I worked for a summer at a nearby hotel on one of the main shopping streets.

Names of Days of the Week, Months, and Holidays

This year, Memorial Day falls on the last Thursday in May.

But Use small letters for the seasons—summer, fall, winter, spring.

In the early summer and fall, my hay fever bothers me.

Names of Commercial Products

The consumer magazine gave high ratings to Cheerios breakfast cereal, Breyer's ice cream, and Progresso chicken noodle soup.

But Use small letters for the *type* of product (breakfast cereal, ice cream, chicken noodle soup, and the like).

Titles of Books, Magazines, Articles, Films, Television Shows, Songs, Poems, Stories, Papers That You Write, and the Like

My oral report was on *The Diary of a Young Girl,* by Anne Frank.

While watching *The Young and the Restless* on television, I thumbed through *Cosmopolitan* magazine and the *New York Times.*

Names of Companies, Associations, Unions, Clubs, Religious and Political Groups, and Other Organizations

A new bill before Congress is opposed by the National Rifle Association.

My wife is Jewish; I am Roman Catholic. We are both members of the Democratic Party.

My parents have life insurance with Prudential, auto insurance with Allstate, and medical insurance with Blue Cross and Blue Shield.

Write a paragraph describing the advertisement shown here so that a person who has never seen it will be able to visualize it and fully understand it. Once you have written your paragraph, check to make sure you have used capital letters properly throughout.

Practice

1

In the sentences that follow, cross out the words that need capitals. Then write the capitalized forms of the words in the space provided. The number of spaces tells you how many corrections to make in each case.

4. The Title of my Paper was "The End of the Civil War." My Instructor did not give me a good Grade for it.

   _____ _____ _____ _____

5. My Friend Jesse said, "People no longer have to go to College and get a Degree in order to find a good job and succeed in Life."

   _____ _____ _____ _____

Collaborative Activity

Editing and Rewriting

Working with a partner, read the short paragraph that follows and mark off the sixteen words with missing capital letters. Then use the space provided to rewrite the passage, adding capital letters where needed. Feel free to discuss the passage quietly with your partner and refer back to the chapter when necessary.

¹Red Riding Hood decided to visit her grandmother in brooklyn. ²Old Mrs. Hood had just been released from bayshore hospital, where she had spent the entire month of september recovering from a broken hip. ³Red Riding Hood's mother gave her daughter a container of campbell's vegetable soup and ritz crackers to bring to Grandma Hood. ⁴Red entered the subway entrance on third avenue, and when the train roared in, she boarded a car. ⁵Suddenly, a young man approached red. ⁶He resembled a wolf with his long, greasy hair and beard, and he said, "what a foxy face you've got, little girl. ⁷I'd like to eat you up." ⁸"Leave me alone," said Red. ⁹"I'm a part-time Guardian angel and I know how to defend myself." ¹⁰When he tried to touch Red, she flipped the new york times she was reading into his face to distract him. ¹¹Then she delivered a quick karate chop with her hand. ¹²the man staggered backward, and an elderly woman then batted him with a large box of reynolds aluminum foil from her shopping bag. ¹³The train entered the station and Red Riding Hood stepped over the wolflike man, who lay groaning on the floor. ¹⁴"Maybe this will teach you to let people ride the subway in peace," she said as she stepped through the doors.

continued

_____

_____

_____

_____

_____

_____

_____

_____

_____

_____

_____

Collaborative Activity

Creating Sentences

Working with a partner, write a sentence (or two) as directed. Pay special attention to capital letters.

1. Write a sentence (or two) about a place you like (or want) to visit. Be sure to include the name of the place, including the city, state, or country where it is located.

2. Write a sentence (or two) in which you state the name of your elementary school, your favorite teacher or subject, and your least favorite teacher or subject.

3. Write a sentence (or two) which includes three brand-name products that you often use. You may begin the sentence with the words, "Three brand-name products I use every day are . . ."

4. Think of the name of your favorite musical artist or performer. Then write a sentence in which you include the musician's name and the title of one of his or her songs.

5. Write a sentence in which you describe something you plan to do two days from now. Be sure to include the date and day of the week in your sentence.

Reflective Activity

1. What would writing be like without capital letters? Use an example or two to help show how capital letters are important to writing.

2. What three uses of capital letters are most difficult for you to remember? Explain, giving examples.

Review Test   1

Cross out the words that need capitals in the following sentences. Then write the capitalized forms of the words in the spaces provided. The number of spaces tells you how many corrections to make in each sentence.

EXAMPLE

During halftime of the ~~saturday~~ afternoon football game, my sister said, "~~let's~~ get some hamburgers from ~~wendy's~~ or put a pizza in the oven."

    Saturday   *Let's*   *Wendy's*

1. Stanley was disgusted when he was told he couldn't order lipton tea at the chinese restaurant.

   _____ _____

2. When my grandfather came to america from the ukraine, which was then a part of russia, he spoke no english.

   _____ _____ _____ _____

3. Nikki said, "i've been working as a waitress at the red lobster since last march."

   _____ _____ _____ _____

4. My math 101 course meets on tuesdays in wister hall.

   _____ _____ _____ _____

5. Every election Day, my mother takes a day off from her job as a nurse at memorial hospital to serve as a poll watcher for the democrats.

   _____ _____ _____ _____

6. "At my age," grandma rose said, "i'm just glad to wake up each morning."

   _____ _____ _____

7. At the corner of thirteenth and market streets is a newsstand where people can buy magazines from as far away as france.

   _____   _____   _____   _____

8. When aunt esther's pontiac finally broke down, she decided to get a toyota.

   _____   _____   _____   _____

9. The college is showing the movie *stagecoach* on friday night as part of its john wayne film festival.

   _____   _____   _____   _____

10. On our trip to washington, we visited the lincoln memorial, sat through a session of the United States senate, and then fell asleep at a concert at the kennedy center.

    _____   _____   _____

    _____   _____   _____

Review Test   2

On separate paper, write

- Seven sentences demonstrating the seven main uses of capital letters.
- Eight sentences demonstrating the eight other uses of capital letters.

NAME: _____

DATE: _____

End Marks   MASTERY TEST 2

Add a period, a question mark, or an exclamation point, as needed, to each of the following sentences.

> **HINT** End marks go *inside* the quotation marks that appear in some sentences.

1. Uncle Arthur's mustache makes him look like a walrus

2. Do coleslaw and French fries come with every order

3. From the airplane window, the clouds looked like mashed potatoes

4. A voice from the stands screamed, "Strike the bum out "

5. How can you hold down two jobs and still go to college

6. With a loud crack, the rotted branch broke and fell from the tree

7. "On your way over," asked Fran, "could you pick up some cheese and crackers "

8. Every time I take a shower, the kitchen ceiling begins to drip

9. The instructor asked me whether I had studied for the exam

10. "Somebody's been squeezing the bottom of the chocolates without eating them " Mariah cried.

11. Annie wanted to know if I had finished bathing the dog

12. Why do I always get thirsty in the middle of the night

13. You're going to knock the vase off the table—watch out

14. I often wonder why more people don't buy live Christmas trees and plant them in their yards afterward

15. Must all our house guests bring screaming kids with them

16. The minute Aunt Agatha thought she had won, she jumped out of her seat and yelled "Bingo "

17. I'd think twice before I took one of his courses again

18. The water company wants to know if it can replace the meter in our basement

19. Have you tried that new Indian fast-food restaurant, Cash and Curry

20. It is better to keep one's mouth closed and be thought a fool than to open it and remove all doubt

Apostrophe

24

Introductory Activity

Carefully look over the three items below. Then see if you can answer the questions that follow each item.

1. She is my best friend.   =   She's my best friend.

    I am afraid of snakes.   =   I'm afraid of snakes.

    Do not watch too much TV. =   Don't watch too much TV.

    They are a perfect match.   =   They're a perfect match.

    It is a terrible movie.   =   It's a terrible movie.

What is the purpose of the apostrophe in the examples above?

_____

_____

2. the desk of the editor   =   the editor's desk

    the car of Giovanni   =   Giovanni's car

    the teeth of my cat   =   my cat's teeth

    the smile of the child   =   the child's smile

    the briefcase of my mother =   my mother's briefcase

What is the purpose of the apostrophe in the examples above?

_____

_____

3. Several families were affected by the flood. One family's car floated away and was found in a field more than a mile away.

    Why does the apostrophe belong in the second sentence but not the first?

    _____

    _____

    Answers are on page 570.

The two main uses of the apostrophe are

1. To show the omission of one or more letters in a contraction
2. To show ownership or possession

Each use is explained on the pages that follow.

Apostrophe in Contractions

A contraction is formed when two words are combined to make one word. An apostrophe is used to show where letters are omitted in forming the contraction. Here are two contractions:

www.mhhe.com/langan

have + not = haven't (the *o* in *not* has been omitted)

I + will = I'll (the *wi* in *will* has been omitted)

The following are some other common contractions:

I + am = I'm	it + is = it's
I + have = I've	it + has = it's
I + had = I'd	is + not = isn't
who + is = who's	could + not = couldn't
do + not = don't	I + would = I'd
did + not = didn't	they + are = they're
let + us = let's	there + is = there's

> **TIP** *will* + *not* has an unusual contraction: *won't*.

Practice 1

Combine the following words into contractions. Two are done for you.

he + is = ___*he's*___		we + are = ___we're___
are + not = ___*isn't*___		has + not = ___*hasn't*___
you + are = ___*you're*___		who + is = ___*who's*___
they + have = ___*they've*___		does + not = ___*doesn't*___
would + not = ___*wouldn't*___		where + is = ___*where's*___

Practice 2

Write the contraction for the words in parentheses.

EXAMPLE

He (could not) ___*couldn't*___ come.

1. (I will) _____ be with you shortly if (you will) _____ just wait a minute.

2. (It is) _____ such a long drive to the ballpark that Luan (would not) _____ go there if you paid him.

3. You (should not) _____ drink any more if (you are) _____ hoping to get home safely.

4. Alisha's husband (is not) _____ the aggressive type, and her former husbands (were not) _____ either.

5. (I would) _____ like to know (who is) _____ in charge of the cash register and why (it is) _____ taking so long for this line to move.

> **TIP** Even though contractions are common in everyday speech and in written dialogue, usually it is best to avoid them in formal writing.

Practice 3

Write five sentences using the apostrophe in different contractions.

1. _____

2. _____

3. _____

4. _____

5. _____

Four Contractions to Note Carefully

Four contractions that deserve special attention are *they're, it's, you're,* and *who's.* Sometimes these contractions are confused with the possessive words *their, its, your,* and *whose.* The list below shows the difference in meaning between the contractions and the possessive words.

Contractions	Possessive Words
they're (means *they are*)	their (means *belonging to them*)
it's (means *it is* or *it has*)	its (means *belonging to it*)
you're (means *you are*)	your (means *belonging to you*)
who's (means *who is*)	whose (means *belonging to whom*)

Possessive words are explained further on page 326.

Underline the correct form (the contraction or the possessive word) in each of the following sentences. Use the contraction whenever the two words of the contraction (*they are, it is, you are, who is*) would also fit.

1. (They're, Their) going to hold the party in (they're, their) family room.

2. (You're, Your) not going to be invited if you insist on bringing (you're, your) accordion.

3. (Who's, Whose) going with us, and (who's, whose) car are we taking?

4. (It's, Its) too early to go to bed and (it's, its) too late in the day to take a nap.

5. If (your, you're) not going to drive by (they're, their) house, (it's, its) going to be impossible for them to get home tonight.

Apostrophe to Show Ownership or Possession

To show ownership or possession, we can use such words as *belongs to, owned by,* or (most commonly) *of.*

the knapsack *that belongs to* Lola

the grades *possessed by* Travis

the house *owned by* my mother

the sore feet *of* the ballet dancer

Practice

4

But the apostrophe plus *s* is often the quickest and easiest way to show possession. Thus we can say:

> Lola's knapsack
>
> Travis's grades
>
> my mother's house
>
> the ballet dancer's sore feet

Points to Remember

1. The *'s* goes with the owner or possessor (in the examples given, *Lola, Travis, mother,* and *dancer*). What follows is the person or thing possessed (in the examples given, *knapsack, grades, house,* and *sore feet*). An easy way to determine the owner or possessor is to ask the question "Who owns it?" In the first example, the answer to the question "Who owns the knapsack?" is *Lola.* Therefore, the *'s* goes with *Lola.*

2. In handwriting, there should always be a break between the word and the *'s.*

Lola's   not   Lola's

Yes   No

3. A singular word ending in *-s* (such as *Travis*) also shows possession by adding an apostrophe plus *s* (Travis's).

Practice	Rewrite the italicized part of each of the sentences below, using the *'s* to show possession. Remember that the *'s* goes with the owner or possessor.
5	**EXAMPLES**

The motorcycle owned by Clyde is a frightening machine.

Clyde's motorcycle

_____

The roommate of my brother is a sweet and friendly person.

My brother's roommate

_____

1. The *sneakers owned by Lola* were stolen.

_____

2. As a joke, he put on *the lipstick that belongs to Veronica.*

_____

3. *The house of his brother* was burglarized.

_____

4. *The tires belonging to the car* are badly worn.

_____

5. *The bicycle owned by Joe* was stolen from the bike rack outside school.

_____

6. I discovered the *nest of the blue jay* while pruning the tree.

_____

7. I don't like *the title of my paper*.

_____

8. *The arthritis of my mother* gets progressively worse.

_____

9. *The boyfriend belonging to my sister* is a gorgeous-looking man.

_____

10. It is *a game belonging to anybody* at this point.

_____

Underline the word in each sentence that needs an *'s*. Then write the word correctly in the space at the left. One is done for you as an example.

6

children's   1. The children voices carried downstairs.

Georgia's   2. Georgia husband is not a take-charge guy.

Friend's   3. My friend computer is also a typewriter.

teacher's   4. When the teacher anger became apparent, the class quickly grew quiet.

girlfriend's   5. His girlfriend apple pie made his stomach rebel.

Albert's   6. Albert dog looks like a porcupine without its quills.

daughter's   7. Under the couch were several of our daughter toys.

bosses   8. My boss car was stolen.

nights   9. That wine tastes like last night rain.

Son's   10. The dentist charged $75 to fix our son tooth.

Add an *'s* to each of the following words to make it the possessor or owner of something. Then write sentences using the words. Your sentences can be serious or playful. One is done for you as an example.

1. Cary _____ *Cary's* _____

   _____ *Cary's hair is bright red.* _____

2. neighbor_____

   _____

3. car _____

   _____

4. sister _____

   _____

5. doctor _____

   _____

Apostrophe versus Possessive Pronouns

Do not use an apostrophe with possessive pronouns. They already show owner-ship. Possessive pronouns include *his, hers, its, yours, ours,* and *theirs.*

Incorrect	Correct
The bookstore lost its' lease.	The bookstore lost its lease.
The racing bikes were theirs'.	The racing bikes were theirs.
The change is yours'.	The change is yours.
His' problems are ours', too.	His problems are ours, too.
Her' cold is worse than his'.	Her cold is worse than his.

Apostrophe versus Simple Plurals

When you want to make a word plural, just add an *s* at the end of the word. Do *not* add an apostrophe. For example, the plural of the word *movie* is *movies,* not *movie's* or *movies'*. Look at this sentence:

   When Korie's cat began catching birds, the neighbors called the police.

The words *birds* and *neighbors* are simple plurals, meaning more than one bird, more than one neighbor. The plural is shown by adding *-s* only. (More information about plurals starts on page 396.) On the other hand, the *'s* after *Korie* shows possession—that Korie owns the cat.

Review Test   2

Rewrite the following sentences, changing the underlined words into either a contraction or a possessive.

1. I do not think the office of Sarita is anything for her to boast about to friends.

   _____

   _____

2. I have been warned by friends about the false charms of Michael.

   _____

   _____

3. The house of the Murphys uses the rays of the sun as a heating source.

   _____

   _____

4. The bill of the plumber was very high, but his work was not very good.

   _____

   _____

5. The menu of the restaurant is not very extensive.

   _____

   _____

NAME: _____

DATE: _____

MASTERY TEST 1 ## Apostrophe

In each sentence, cross out the word that needs an apostrophe. Then write the word correctly in the space provided.

_____ 1. I walked casually around the parking lot, trying to conceal the fact that Id no idea where I left my car.

_____ 2. Thea ignored the police motorcycle officers siren and ended up in jail last night.

_____ 3. The man insisted that his name was Elmer Fudd, but I didnt believe him.

_____ 4. The blue whales tongue weighs about as much as forty men.

_____ 5. Lolas mother put on some old jeans and helped Lola paint her new apartment.

_____ 6. Tony had to remove wood ticks from his hair after a walk through the field behind his uncles house.

_____ 7. The womens room in that service station is always clean.

_____ 8. Youre going to cause trouble for yourself if your temper gets out of hand.

_____ 9. Some of the most violent crime years in our nations history occurred during the Great Depression.

_____ 10. Because Russias population is declining, many of its small towns are gradually being abandoned.

NAME: _____

DATE: _____

Apostrophe MASTERY TEST 2

In the space provided under each sentence, add the one apostrophe needed and explain why the other word ending in *s* is a simple plural.

EXAMPLE

Joans hair began to fall out two days after she dyed it.

Joans: *Joan's meaning "hair belonging to Joan"*

days: *simple plural meaning more than one day*

1. The students gradually got used to the professors Japanese accent.

   students: _____

   professors: _____

2. Our tough sheriffs campaign promise is that he'll replace the electric chair with electric bleachers.

   sheriffs: _____

   bleachers: _____

3. My little sisters habit of sucking in noodles makes her an unpleasant dining companion.

   sisters: _____

   noodles: _____

4. When the students complained about the instructors assignment, he said, "You're not in high school anymore."

   students: _____

   instructors: _____

5. A football-sized nest of yellow jackets hung menacingly under the roofs rain gutter.

   jackets: _____

   roofs: _____

MASTERY TEST 3 | Apostrophe

In each sentence two apostrophes are missing or are used incorrectly. Cross out the two errors and write the corrections in the spaces provided.

Terrences'

1. Terrences day started going sour when he noticed that everyone in the donut shop had gotten fatter donuts' than he got.

Showers'
Players'

2. While the team was in the showers, someone tied all the players sneakers' together.

you'll
I'll

3. If youll check the noise in the attic, Ill stand by the phone in case you scream.

drivers'
Cigarettes

4. Despite the drivers warning that smoking was not allowed, several people lit cigarettes' in the back of the bus.

Hassan's
darts

5. When I sat on the fender of Hassans car, he stared darts' at me until I slid off.

brothers'
Vandals

6. My brothers cell phone was stolen by vandals' who broke his car window.

Melissas'
She'd

7. Melissas typing might improve if shed cut an inch off her nails.

Andy's
his

8. Anna has been on Andys blacklist since she revealed that he sleeps with his' socks on.

trooper's
drivers'

9. The troopers face was stern as he told me that my drivers license had expired.

uncle's
it's

10. I never ride anymore in my uncles station wagon; its like being on a roller coaster.

336

Apostrophe MASTERY TEST 4

In each sentence two apostrophes are missing or are used incorrectly. Cross out the two errors and write the corrections in the spaces provided.

_____
_____

1. I was shocked when the movie stars toupee blew off; I hadnt realized he was completely bald.

_____
_____

2. The skirts cheap lining puckered and scorched even though Eileens iron was set at the lowest possible heat level.

_____
_____

3. The two boys boat capsized in the rivers rushing current.

_____
_____

4. Teds work always ends up on someone elses desk.

_____
_____

5. People in the dentists waiting room squirmed uneasily as a childs cries echoed down the hall.

_____
_____

6. When Jeans voice cracked during her solo, I thought shed faint with embarrassment.

_____
_____

7. Didnt you know that school will be closed next week because of a teachers conference?

_____
_____

8. My youngest sisters goldfish has jumped out of its' bowl many times.

_____
_____

9. "Its the muffler," the mechanic explained, crawling out from under Freds car.

_____
_____

10. Kevin knew he was headed for trouble when his dates father said that hed like to come along.

Quotation Marks

Introductory Activity

Read the following scene and underline all the words enclosed within quotation marks. Your instructor may also have you dramatize the scene with one person reading the narration and three persons acting the speaking parts—Len, Tina, and Mario. The two speakers should imagine the scene as part of a stage play and try to make their words seem as real and true-to-life as possible.

At a party that Len and his wife Tina recently hosted, Len got angry at a guy named Mario who kept bothering Tina. "Listen, man," Len said, "what's this thing you have for my wife? There are lots of other women at this party."

"Relax," Mario replied. "Tina is very attractive, and I enjoy talking with her."

"Listen, Mario," Tina said. "I've already told you three times that I don't want to talk to you anymore. Please leave me alone."

"Look, there's no law that says I can't talk to you if I want to," Mario challenged.

"Mario, I'm only going to say this once," Len warned. "Lay off my wife, or leave this party *now*."

Mario grinned at Len smugly. "You've got good liquor here. Why should I leave? Besides, I'm not done talking with Tina."

Len went to his basement and was back a minute later holding a two-by-four. "I'm giving you a choice," Len said. "Leave by the door or I'll slam you out the window."

Mario left by the door.

4. Lynn exclaimed that Eric was crazy.

   _____

5. Eric replied that she had much better handwriting than he did.

   _____

Rewrite the following sentences, converting each direct quotation into an indirect statement. In each case you will have to add the word *that* or *if* and change other words as well.

EXAMPLE

The barber asked Reggie, "Have you noticed how your hair is thinning?"

The barber asked Reggie if he had noticed how his hair was thinning.

1. He said, "As the plane went higher, my heart sank lower."

   _____

2. The designer said, "Shag rugs are back in style."

   _____

3. The foreman asked Susan, "Have you ever operated a lift truck?"

   _____

4. My new neighbor asked, "Would you like to come over for coffee?"

   _____

5. Mei Lin complained, "I married a man who eats Tweeties cereal for breakfast."

   _____

   _____

Quotation Marks to Set Off the Titles of Short Works

www.mhhe.com/langan

Titles of short works are usually set off by quotation marks, while titles of long works are underlined. Use quotation marks to set off the titles of such short works as articles in books, newspapers, or magazines; chapters in a book; short stories; poems; and songs. On the other hand, you should underline the titles of books, newspapers, magazines, plays, movies, compact discs, and television shows. See the following examples.

Quotation Marks	Underlines
the article "The Toxic Tragedy"	in the book <u>Who's Poisoning America</u>
the article "New Cures for Head-aches"	in the newspaper <u>The New York Times</u>
the article "When the Patient Plays Doctor"	in the magazine <u>Family Health</u>
	in the book <u>Straight Talk</u>
the chapter "Connecting with Kids"	in the book <u>Dubliners</u>
the story "The Dead"	in the book <u>The Complete Poems of Robert Frost</u>
the poem "Birches"	in the album <u>South Pacific</u>
the song "Some Enchanted Evening"	the television show <u>Jeopardy</u>
	the movie <u>Rear Window</u>

> **TIP** In printed form, the titles of long works are set off by italics—slanted type that looks *like this*.

Practice 6

Use quotation marks or underlines as needed.

1. The young couple opened their brand-new copy of Cooking Made Easy to the chapter titled Meat Loaf Magic.

2. Annabelle borrowed Hawthorne's novel The Scarlet Letter from the library because she thought it was about a varsity athlete.

3. Did you know that the musical West Side Story is actually a modern version of Shakespeare's tragedy Romeo and Juliet?

4. I used to think that Richard Connell's short story The Most Dangerous Game was the scariest piece of suspense fiction in existence—until I began reading Bram Stoker's classic novel Dracula.

5. Every year at Easter, we watch a movie such as The Robe on television.

6. During the past year, Time featured an article about DNA titled Building Blocks of the Future.

7. My father still remembers the way Sarah Brightman sang "Think of Me" in the original production of The Phantom of the Opera.

8. As I stand in the supermarket checkout line, I read a feature story in the National Enquirer titled Mother Gives Birth to Alien Baby.

9. My favorite song by Aretha Franklin is the classic Respect, which has been included in the CD Aretha's Best.

10. Absentmindedly munching a Dorito, Hana opened the latest issue of Newsweek to its cover story, The Junk Food Explosion.

Other Uses of Quotation Marks

1. **To set off special words or phrases from the rest of a sentence:**

   Many people spell the words "all right" as one word, "alright," instead of correctly spelling them as two words.

   I have trouble telling the difference between "principal" and "principle."

2. **To mark off a quote within a quote. For this purpose, single quotes (' ') are used:**

   Ben Franklin said, "The noblest question in the world is, 'What good may I do in it?'"

   "If you want to have a scary experience," Eric told Lynn, "read Stephen King's story 'The Mangler' in his book *Night Shift*."

Collaborative Activity

Editing and Rewriting

Working with a partner, read the short passage below and circle the ten sets of quotation mark mistakes. Then use the space provided to rewrite the passage, adding the ten sets of quotation marks. Feel free to discuss the rewrite quietly with your partner and refer back to the chapter when necessary.

¹Holding a container of milk and a bag of potatoes, Tony and Lola were standing in the express line at the Safeway supermarket. ²Lola pointed to a sign above the checkout counter that read, Express line— ten items or less. ³She then said to Tony, Look at that guy ahead of us. ⁴He shouldn't be in the express lane.

⁵Be quiet, said Tony. ⁶If you're not, he'll hear you.

⁷I don't mind if he does hear me, Lola replied. ⁸People like that think the world owes them a favor. ⁹I hope the cashier makes him go to another lane. ¹⁰The man in front of them suddenly turned around. ¹¹Stop acting as if I've committed a federal crime, he said. ¹²See those five cans of Alpo—that counts as one item. ¹³See those four packs of Twinkies—that's one item. ¹⁴Let's just say this, Lola replied. ¹⁵You have an interesting way of counting.

_____

_____

_____

_____

_____

_____

_____

_____

_____

_____

_____

_____

Collaborative Activity

Creating Sentences

Working with a partner, write sentences that use quotation marks as directed.

1. Write a sentence in which you quote a favorite expression of someone you know. Identify the person's relationship to you.

   EXAMPLE

   My brother Sam often says after a meal, "That wasn't bad at all."

   _____

   _____

   _____

2. Write a quotation that contains the words *Tony asked Lola*. Write a second quotation that includes the words *Lola replied*.

   _____

   _____

   _____

3. Write a sentence that interests or amuses you from a book, magazine, or newspaper. Identify the title and author of the book, magazine, or newspaper article.

   EXAMPLE

   In her book <u>At Wit's End</u>, Erma Bombeck advises, "Never go to a doctor whose office plants have died."

   _____

   _____

   _____

Reflective Activity

1. Look at the passage about the checkout line that you revised above. Explain how adding quotation marks has affected the reading of the passage.

2. What would writing be like without quotation marks? Explain, using an example, how quotation marks are important to understanding writing.

3. Explain what it is about quotation marks that is most difficult for you to remember and apply. Use an example to make your point clear. Feel free to refer back to anything in this chapter.

Review Test 1

Place quotation marks around the exact words of a speaker or writer in the sentences that follow.

1. Are you seeing what I'm seeing? the friends asked each other.

2. Murphy's law states, Whatever can go wrong, will.

3. John Kennedy once said, Ask not what your country can do for you; ask what you can do for your country.

4. The sign read, Be careful how you drive. You may meet a fool.

5. Martha said, Turn on the burglar alarm when you leave the house, Fred.

6. Tony asked the struggling old lady if he could help with her heavy bag. Go to blazes, you masher, she said.

7. Listen, I confided to my sister, Neil told me he is going to ask you to go out with him.

8. The sign in the tough Western saloon read, Carry out your own dead.

9. When the ball hit Willie Wilson in the head and bounced into the outfield, Eric remarked, That was a heads-up play.

10. A woman who was one of Winston Churchill's political enemies once remarked to him, If you were my husband, I would put poison in your coffee. Churchill's reply was, Madam, if I were your husband, I would drink it.

Review Test 2

Go through the comics section of a newspaper to find a comic strip that amuses you. Be sure to choose a strip where two or more characters are speaking to each other. Write a full description that will enable people who have not read the comic strip to visualize it clearly and appreciate its humor. Describe the setting and action in each panel and enclose the words of the speakers in quotation marks.

MASTERY TEST 1   # Quotation Marks

Place quotation marks where needed.

1. A friend of mine used to say, There's nothing wrong with you that a few birthdays won't cure.

2. The food critic wrote, The best test of a fast-food hamburger is to eat it after all the trimmings have been taken off.

3. After I finished James Thurber's story The Secret Life of Walter Mitty, I started to write a paper on it.

4. Poet and writer Maya Angelou said, When people show you who they are, believe them.

5. Well, this is just fine, he mumbled. The recipe calls for four eggs and I have only two.

6. Eating Lola's chili, Tony whispered, is a breathtaking experience.

7. After Bill pulled the flip-top cap off the can, he noticed that the label said, Shake well before drinking.

8. How would you feel, the instructor asked the class, if I gave you a surprise quiz today?

9. In a tired voice, Clyde asked, Did you ever wonder why kids have more energy at the end of a long day than they had when they got up?

10. When Dick Cavett first met Groucho Marx on a street corner, he said, Hello, Groucho, I'm a big fan of yours. Groucho's response was, If it gets any hotter, I could use a big fan.

_____ 6. Kyle has driven 1,500,000 accident-free miles in his job as a trucker.

The Wynn Trucking Company of Jersey City, New Jersey, gave Kyle an award on September 26, 2009, for his superior safety record.

> a. separate items in a list
> b. separate introductory material from the sentence
> c. separate words that interrupt the sentence
> d. separate complete thoughts in a sentence
> e. separate direct quotations from the rest of the sentence
> f. separate numbers, addresses, and dates in everyday writing

Answers are on page 572.

www.mhhe.com/langan

Six Main Uses of the Comma

Commas are used mainly as follows:

1. To separate items in a series

2. To set off introductory material

3. On both sides of words that interrupt the flow of thought in a sentence

4. Between two complete thoughts connected by *and, but, for, or, nor, so, yet*

5. To set off a direct quotation from the rest of a sentence

6. For certain everyday material

You may find it helpful to remember that the comma often marks a slight pause, or break, in a sentence. These pauses or breaks occur at the points where the six main comma rules apply. Read aloud the sentence examples given on the following pages for each of the comma rules and listen for the minor pauses or breaks that are signaled by commas.

At the same time, you should keep in mind that commas are far more often overused than underused. As a general rule, you should *not* use a comma unless a given comma rule applies or unless a comma is otherwise needed to help a sentence read clearly. A good rule of thumb is that "when in doubt" about whether to use a comma, it is often best to "leave it out."

After reviewing each of the comma rules that follow, you will practice adding commas that are needed and omitting commas that are not needed.

Comma between Items in a Series

Use a comma to separate items in a series.

Magazines, paperback novels, and textbooks crowded the shelves.

Hard-luck Harold needs a loan, a good-paying job, and a close friend.

Pat sat in the doctor's office, checked her watch, and chewed gum nervously.

Lola bit into the ripe, juicy apple.

More and more people entered the crowded, noisy stadium.

A comma is used between two descriptive words in a series only if *and* inserted between the words sounds natural. You could say:

Lola bit into the ripe *and* juicy apple.

More and more people entered the crowded *and* noisy stadium.

But notice in the following sentences that the descriptive words do not sound natural when *and* is inserted between them. In such cases, no comma is used.

The model wore a light sleeveless blouse. ("A light *and* sleeveless blouse" doesn't sound right, so no comma is used.)

Dr. Van Helsing noticed two tiny puncture marks on his patient's neck. ("Two *and* tiny puncture marks" doesn't sound right, so no comma is used.)

Practice 1

Place commas between items in a series.

1. Becky brought a cake iced with red white and blue frosting to the Fourth of July picnic.

2. My brother did the laundry helped clean the apartment waxed the car and watched an old episode of HBO's *The Sopranos.*

3. You can make a Big Mac by putting two all-beef patties special sauce lettuce cheese pickles and onions on a sesame-seed bun.

Practice 2

For each item, cross out the one comma that is not needed. Add the one comma that is needed between items in a series.

1. Cold eggs burnt bacon and watery orange juice are the reasons, I've never returned to that diner for breakfast.

2. Andy relaxes, by reading Donald Duck Archie, and Bugs Bunny comic books.

3. Tonight I've got to work at the restaurant for three hours finish writing a paper, and study, for an exam.

SECTION 4:
PUNCTUATION AND
MECHANICS

Comma after Introductory Material

Use a comma to set off introductory material.

Fearlessly, Lola picked up the slimy slug.

Just to annoy Tony, she let it crawl along her arm.

Although I have a black belt in karate, I decided to go easy on the demented bully who had kicked sand in my face.

Mumbling under her breath, the woman picked over the tomatoes.

TIPS

a. If the introductory material is brief, the comma is sometimes omitted. In the activities here, however, you should include the comma.

b. A comma is also used to set off extra material placed at the end of a sentence. Here are two sentences where this comma rule applies:

I spent all day at the employment office, trying to find a job that suited me.

Tony has trouble accepting criticism, except from Lola.

Place commas after introductory material.

Practice

3

1. When I didn't get my paycheck at work I called up the business office. According to the office computer I was dead.

2. After seeing the accident Susan wanted to stop driving forever. Even so she went driving to work next morning over the ice-covered roads.

3. To get her hair done Faye goes to a beauty salon all the way across town. Once there she enjoys listening to the gossip in the beauty shop. Also she likes looking through *Elle* and other magazines in the shop.

For each item, cross out the one comma that is not needed. Add the one comma that is needed after introductory material.

Practice

4

1. Even though Tina had an upset stomach she went bowling, with her husband.

2. Looking back over the last ten years I can see several decisions I made, that really changed my life.

3. Instead of going with my family to the mall I decided to relax at home, and to call up some friends.

Comma around Words Interrupting the Flow of Thought

Use a comma before and after words that interrupt the flow of thought in a sentence.

> The car, cleaned and repaired, is ready to be sold.
>
> Joanne, our new neighbor, used to work as a bouncer at Rexy's Tavern.
>
> Taking long walks, especially after dark, helps me sort out my thoughts.

Usually you can "hear" words that interrupt the flow of thought in a sentence. However, when you are not sure if certain words are interrupters, remove them from the sentence. If it still makes sense without the words, you know the words are interrupters and that the information they give is nonessential. Such nonessential information is set off with commas. Consider the following sentence:

> Susie Hall, who is my best friend, won a new car in the *Reader's Digest* sweepstakes.

Here the words *who is my best friend* are extra information, not needed to identify the subject of the sentence, *Susie Hall.* Put commas around such nonessential information. Contrast that sentence with this one:

> The woman who is my best friend won a new car in the *Reader's Digest* sweepstakes.

Here the words *who is my best friend* supply essential information needed for us to identify the woman. If the words were removed from the sentence, we would no longer know which woman won the sweepstakes. Commas are not used around such essential information.

Here is another example:

> *The Shining,* a novel by Stephen King, is the scariest book I've ever read.

Here the words *a novel by Stephen King* are extra information, not needed to identify the subject of the sentence, *The Shining.* Commas go around such nonessential information. Here's a similar sentence without the commas:

> Stephen King's novel *The Shining* is the scariest book I've ever read.

Here the words *The Shining* are needed to identify the novel. Commas are not used around such essential information.

Most of the time you will be able to "hear" words that interrupt the flow of thoughts in a sentence and will not have to think about whether the words are essential or nonessential.*

---

*Some instructors refer to nonessential or extra information that is set off by commas as a *nonrestrictive* clause. Essential information that interrupts the flow of thought is called a *restrictive* clause. No commas are used to set off a restrictive clause.

Add commas to set off interrupting words.

1. Friday is the deadline the absolute final deadline for your papers to be turned in.

2. The nursery rhyme told how the cow a weird creature jumped over the moon. The rhyme also related how the dish who must also have been strange ran away with the spoon.

3. Tod voted the most likely to succeed in our high school graduating class has just made the front page of our newspaper. He was arrested with other members of the King Kongs a local motorcycle gang for creating a disturbance in the park.

For each item, cross out the one comma that is not needed. Add the two commas that are needed to set off interrupting words.

1. My sister's cat which she got from the animal shelter woke her, when her apartment caught fire.

2. A bulging biology textbook its pages stuffed with notes, and handouts lay on the path to the college parking lot.

3. A baked potato with its crispy skin and soft inside rates as one of my all-time favorite, foods.

Comma between Complete Thoughts Connected by a Joining Word

Use a comma between two complete thoughts connected by *and, but, for, or, nor, so, yet.*

> My parents threatened to throw me out of the house, so I had to stop playing the drums.

> The polyester bed sheets had a gorgeous design on them, but they didn't feel as comfortable as plain cotton sheets.

> The teenage girls walked the hot summer streets, and the teenage boys drove by in their shined-up cars.

The comma is optional when the complete thoughts are short:

> Calvin relaxed but Robert kept working.

> The soda was flat so I poured it away.

> We left school early for the furnace broke down.

Be careful not to use a comma in sentences having *one* subject and a *double* verb. The comma is used only in sentences made up of two complete thoughts (two subjects and two verbs). In the sentence

Tamika lay awake that stormy night and listened to the thunder crashing

there is only one subject (*Dawn*) and a double verb (*lay* and *listened*). No comma is needed. Likewise, the sentence

The quarterback kept the ball and plunged across the goal line for a touch-down

has only one subject (*quarterback*) and a double verb (*kept* and *plunged*); there-fore, no comma is needed.

Practice

7

Place a comma before a joining word that connects two complete thoughts (two subjects and two verbs). The four sentences that have only one subject and a double verb do not need commas; mark these *C* for "correct."

1. The outfielder raced to the warning track and caught the fly ball over his shoulder.
2. The sun set in a golden glow behind the mountain and a single star sparkled in the night sky.
3. Arturo often tries to cut back on his eating but he always gives up after a few days.
4. Her voice became very dry during the long speech and beads of perspiration began to appear on her forehead.
5. Cheryl learned two computer languages in high school and then began writing her own programs.
6. I spent all of Saturday morning trying to fix my car but I still wound up taking it to a garage in the afternoon.
7. She felt like shouting but didn't dare open her mouth.
8. He's making a good living selling cosmetics to beauty shops but he still has regrets about not having gone to college.
9. Crazy Bill often goes into bars and asks people to buy him a drink.
10. He decided not to take the course in advanced math for he wanted to have time for a social life during the semester.

Comma with Direct Quotations

Use a comma to set off a direct quotation from the rest of a sentence.

"Please take a number," said the deli clerk.

Fred told Martha, "I've just signed up for a Dale Carnegie course."

"Those who sling mud," a famous politician once said, "usually lose ground."

"Reading this book," complained Francesca, "is about as interesting as watching paint dry."

TIP A comma or a period at the end of a quotation goes inside quotation marks. See also pages 339–340.

In each sentence, add the one or more commas needed to set off the quoted material.

Practice 8

1. "I can't wait to have a fish filet and some fries" said Lola to Tony as she pulled into the order lane at the fast-food restaurant. She asked "What can I get you, Tony?"

2. "Two quarter-pounders with cheese, two large fries, and a large Coke" responded Tony.

3. "Good grief" said Lola. "It's hard to believe you don't weigh three hundred pounds. In fact" she continued "how much do you weigh?"

In each item, cross out the one comma that is not needed to set off a quotation. Add the comma that is needed to set off a quotation from the rest of the sentence.

Practice 9

1. "You better hurry" Thelma's mother warned "or you're going to miss the last bus, of the morning."

2. "It really worries me" said Marty "that you haven't seen a doctor, about that strange swelling under your arm."

3. The student sighed in frustration, and then raised his hand. "My computer has crashed again" he called out to the instructor.

Comma with Everyday Material

Use a comma with certain everyday material as shown in the following sections.

Persons Spoken To

Sally, I think that you should go to bed.

Please turn down the stereo, Mark.

Please, sir, can you spare a dollar?

Dates

My best friend got married on April 29, 2005, and he became a parent on January 7, 2007.

Addresses

Lola's sister lives at Greenway Village, 342 Red Oak Drive, Los Angeles, California 90057.

> **TIP** No comma is used before the zip code.

Openings and Closings of Letters

Dear Vanessa,	Sincerely,
Dear John,	Truly yours,

> **TIP** In formal letters, a colon is used after the opening:
>
> Dear Sir:
>
> Dear Madam:

Numbers

Government officials estimate that Americans spend about 785,000,000 hours a year filling out federal forms.

Practice 10

Place commas where needed.

1. I am sorry sir but you cannot sit at this table.

2. On May 6 1954 Roger Bannister became the first person to run a mile in under four minutes.

3. Redeeming the savings certificate before June 30 2010 will result in a substantial penalty.

4. A cash refund of one dollar can be obtained by sending proof of purchase to Seven Seas P.O. Box 760 El Paso TX 79972.

5. Leo get out of bed and come to the lecture with me!

Unnecessary Use of Commas

Remember that if no clear rule applies for using a comma, it is usually better not to use a comma. As stated earlier, "When in doubt, leave it out." Following are some typical examples of unnecessary commas.

Incorrect

Sharon told me, that my socks were different colors. (A comma is not used before *that* unless the flow of thought is interrupted.)

The union negotiations, dragged on for three days. (Do not use a comma between a simple subject and verb.)

I waxed all the furniture, and cleaned the windows. (Use a comma before *and* only with more than two items in a series or when *and* joins two complete thoughts.)

Sharon carried, the baby into the house. (Do not use a comma between a verb and its object.)

I had a clear view, of the entire robbery. (Do not use a comma before a prepositional phrase.)

Cross out the one comma that does not belong in each sentence. Do not add any commas.

Practice

11

1. When I arrived to help with the moving, Jerome said to me, that the work was already done.

2. After the flour and milk have been mixed, eggs must be added, to the recipe.

3. Because my sister is allergic to cat fur, and dust, our family does not own a cat or have any dust-catching drapes or rugs.

4. The guys on the corner, asked, "Have you ever taken karate lessons?"

5. As the heavy Caterpillar tractor, rumbled up the street, our house windows rattled.

6. Las Vegas, Miami Beach, San Diego, and Atlantic City, are the four places she has worked as a bartender.

7. Thomas Farley, the handsome young man, who just took off his trousers, recently escaped from an institution for the mentally ill.

8. Hal wanted to go to medical school, but he does not have the money, and was not offered a scholarship.

9. Joyce reads, a lot of fiction, but I prefer stories that really happened.

10. Because Mary is single, her married friends do not invite her, to their parties.

Collaborative Activity

Editing and Rewriting

Working with a partner, read carefully the short paragraph below and cross out the five misplaced commas. Then, in the space between the lines, insert the ten additional commas needed. Feel free to discuss the rewrite quietly with your partner and refer back to the chapter when necessary.

[1]If you want to become a better note-taker you should keep in mind the following hints. [2]Most important you should attend class on a regular basis. [3]The instructor will probably develop in class, all the main ideas of the course and you want to be there to write the ideas down. [4]Students often ask "How much, should I write down?" [5]By paying close attention in class you will probably develop an instinct for the material, that you must write down. [6]You should record your notes in outline form. [7]Start main points at the margin indent major supporting details and further indent more subordinate material. [8]When the speaker moves from one aspect of a topic to another show this shift on your paper, by skipping a line or two. [9]A last hint but by no means the least is to write down any points your instructor repeats or takes the time, to put on the board.

Collaborative Activity

Creating Sentences

Working with a partner, write sentences that use commas as directed.

1. Write a sentence mentioning three items that can be found in the photo.

   _____

   _____

2. Write two sentences describing how you relax after getting home from school or work. Start the first sentence with *After* or *When.* Start the second sentence with *Next.*

   _____

   _____

3. Write a sentence that tells something about your favorite movie, book, television show, or song. Use the words *which is my favorite movie* (or *book, television show,* or *song*) after the name of the movie, book, television show, or song.

   _____

   _____

4. Write two complete thoughts about a person you know. The first thought should mention something that you like about the person. The second thought should mention something you don't like. Join the two thoughts with *but.*

   _____

   _____

5. Invent a line that Lola might say to Tony. Use the words *Lola said* in the sentence. Then include Tony's reply, using the words *Tony responded.*

   _____

   _____

6. Write a sentence about an important event in your life. Include in your sentence the day, month, and year of the event.

   _____

   _____

Reflective Activity

1. Look at the paragraph on note taking that you revised above. Explain how adding commas has affected the reading of the paragraph.

2. What would writing be like without the comma? How do commas help writing?

3. What is the most difficult comma rule for you to remember and apply? Explain, giving an example.

Review Test 1

Insert commas where needed. In the space provided under each sentence, summarize briefly the rule that explains the use of the comma or commas.

1. After I fell and fractured my wrist I decided to sell my skateboard.

   _____

2. She asked her son "Are you going to church with me tomorrow?"

   _____

3. The weather bureau predicts that sleet fire or brimstone will fall on Washington today.

   _____

4. The ignition system in his car as well as the generator was not working properly.

   _____

5. Tony asked Lola "Have you ever had nightmares in which some kind of monster was ready to swallow you?"

   _____

6. They attacked their bathroom with Lysol Comet and Fantastik.

   _____

7. The pan of bacon fat heating on the stove burst into flame and he quickly set a lid on the pan to put out the fire.

   _____

Dictionary Use **MASTERY TEST 1**

ITEMS **1–5**

Use your dictionary to answer the following questions.

1. How many syllables are in the word *decontaminate?* _____

2. Where is the primary accent in the word *interpretation?* _____

3. In the word *posterity,* the *i* is pronounced like

   a. short *e.*

   b. short *i.*

   c. long *i.*

   d. schwa.

4. In the word *secularize,* the *u* is pronounced like

   a. schwa.

   b. short *a.*

   c. short *u.*

   d. long *u.*

5. In the word *erratic,* the *e* is pronounced like

   a. short *e.*

   b. long *e.*

   c. short *i.*

   d. schwa.

ITEMS **6–10**

There are five misspelled words in the following sentence. Cross out each misspelled word and write in the correct spelling in the spaces provided.

The canidate for mayor promised to reduce subway fares by a nickle, to crack down on criminels, and to bring new businesses to the city by ofering tax breaks.

6. _____   8. _____   10. _____

7. _____   9. _____

NAME: _____

DATE: _____

MASTERY TEST 2 ## Dictionary Use

ITEMS 1–5

Use your dictionary to answer the following questions.

1. How many syllables are in the word *rationalize?*_____

2. Where is the primary accent in the word *dilapidated?*_____

3. In the word *vicarious,* the second *i* is pronounced like

    a. long *e.*

    b. short *i.*

    c. long *i.*

    d. schwa.

4. In the word *cumbersome,* the *o* is pronounced like

    a. schwa.

    b. short *a.*

    c. short *o.*

    d. long *o.*

5. In the word *esoteric,* the second *e* is pronounced like

    a. short *e.*

    b. long *e.*

    c. short *i.*

    d. schwa.

ITEMS 6–10

There are five misspelled words in the following sentence. Cross out each misspelled word and write the correct spelling in the space provided.

My mother's most precious possesion is her collection of crystel animals; she keeps them in a specal cabinet in the dineing room and won't allow anyone to handel them.

6. _____   8. _____   10. _____

7. _____   9. _____

Spelling Improvement

29

Introductory Activity

See if you can circle the word that is misspelled in each of the following pairs:

akward	*or*	awkward
exercise	*or*	exercize
business	*or*	buisness
worried	*or*	worryed
shamful	*or*	shameful
begining	*or*	beginning
partys	*or*	parties
sandwichs	*or*	sandwiches
heroes	*or*	heros

Answers are on page 573.

Poor spelling often results from bad habits developed in the early school years. With work, such habits can be corrected. If you can write your name without misspelling it, there is no reason why you can't do the same with almost any word in the English language. Following are seven steps you can take to improve your spelling.

Step 1: Using the Dictionary

Get into the habit of using the dictionary. When you write a paper, allow yourself time to look up the spelling of all the words you are unsure about. Do not underestimate the value of this step just because it is such a simple one. By using the dictionary, you can probably make yourself a 95 percent better speller.

Step 2: Keeping a Personal Spelling List

Keep a list of words you misspell and study those words regularly.

> **TIP**
>
> When you have trouble spelling long words, try to break each word into syllables and see whether you can spell the syllables. For example, *misdemeanor* can be spelled easily if you can hear and spell in turn its four syllables: *mis-de-mean-or*. The word *formidable* can be spelled easily if you hear and spell in turn its four syllables: *for-mi-da-ble*. Remember, then: try to see, hear, and spell long words in terms of their syllables.

Step 3: Mastering Commonly Confused Words

Master the meanings and spellings of the commonly confused words on pages 411–430. Your instructor may assign twenty words for you to study at a time and give you a series of quizzes until you have mastered all the words.

Step 4: Using a Computer's Spell-Checker

Most word-processing programs feature a *spell-checker* that will identify incorrect words and suggest correct spellings. If you are unsure how to use yours, consult the program's "help" function. Spell-checkers are not foolproof; they will fail to catch misused homonyms like the words *your* and *you're*.

Step 5:
Understanding Basic
Spelling Rules

Explained briefly here are three rules that may improve your spelling. While exceptions sometimes occur, these rules hold true most of the time.

1. **Changing y to i.**

   When a word ends in a consonant plus *y,* change *y* to *i* when you add an ending.

try + ed = tried	marry + es = marries
worry + es = worries	lazy + ness = laziness
lucky + ly = luckily	silly + est = silliest

2. **Final silent e.**

   Drop a final *e* before an ending that starts with a vowel (the vowels are *a, e, i, o,* and *u*).

hope + ing = hoping	sense + ible = sensible
fine + est = finest	hide + ing = hiding

   Keep the final *e* before an ending that starts with a consonant.

use + ful = useful	care + less = careless
life + like = lifelike	settle + ment = settlement

3. **Doubling a final consonant.**

   Double the final consonant of a word when all the following are true:

   a. The word is one syllable or is accented on the last syllable.
   b. The word ends in a single consonant preceded by a single vowel.
   c. The ending you are adding starts with a vowel.

sob + ing = sobbing	big + est = biggest
drop + ed = dropped	omit + ed = omitted
admit + ing = admitting	begin + ing = beginning

Combine the following words and endings by applying the three rules above.

1. study + ed = _____
2. advise + ing = _____
3. carry + es = _____
4. stop + ing = _____
5. terrify + ed = _____

6. compel + ed = _____
7. retire + ing = _____
8. hungry + ly = _____
9. expel + ing = _____
10. judge + es = _____

Step 6: Understanding Plurals

Most words form their plurals by adding -*s* to the singular.

Singular	Plural
blanket	blankets
pencil	pencils
street	streets

Some words, however, form their plurals in special ways, as shown in the rules that follow.

1. **Words ending in -*s*, -*ss*, -*z*, -*x*, -*sh*, or -*ch* usually form the plural by adding -*es*.**

kiss	kisses	inch	inches
box	boxes	dish	dishes

2. **Words ending in a consonant plus *y* form the plural by changing *y* to *i* and adding -*es*.**

party	parties	county	counties
baby	babies	city	cities

3. **Some words ending in *f* change the *f* to *v* and add -*es* in the plural.**

leaf	leaves	life	lives
wife	wives	yourself	yourselves

4. **Some words ending in *o* form their plurals by adding -*es*.**

potato	potatoes	mosquito	mosquitoes
hero	heroes	tomato	tomatoes

5. **Some words of foreign origin have irregular plurals. When in doubt, check your dictionary.**

antenna   antennae   crisis   crises
criterion criteria   medium   media

6. **Some words form their plurals by changing letters within the word.**

man   men   foot   feet
tooth teeth   goose   geese

7. **Combined words (words made up of two or more words) form their plurals by adding -s to the main word.**

brother-in-law   brothers-in-law
passerby   passersby

Complete these sentences by filling in the plural of the word at the left.

Practice

2

grocery   1. I carried six bags of _____ into the house.

town   2. How many _____ did you visit during the tour?

policy   3. The president's new _____ are making many voters angry.

body   4. Because the grave diggers were on strike, _____ piled up in the morgue.

lottery   5. She plays two state _____ in hopes of winning a fortune.

pass   6. Hank caught six _____ in a losing cause.

tragedy   7. That woman has had to endure many _____ in her life.

watch   8. I have found that cheap _____ work better for me than expensive ones.

suit   9. To help himself feel better, he went out and bought two _____.

boss   10. I have not one but two _____ to worry about every day.

Step 7: Mastering a Basic Word List

Make sure you can spell all the words in the following list. They are some of the words used most often in English. Again, your instructor may assign twenty words for you to study at a time and give you a series of quizzes until you have mastered the words.

ability	bargain	daily
absent	beautiful	danger
accident	because	daughter
across	become	death
address	before	decide
advertise	begin	deposit
advice	being	describe
after	believe	different
again	between	direction
against	bottom **40**	distance
all right	breathe	doubt
almost	building	dozen
a lot	business	during
although	careful	each
always	careless	early
among	cereal	earth
angry	certain	education
animal	change	either
another	cheap	English
answer **20**	chief	enough **80**
anxious	children	entrance
apply	church	everything
approve	cigarette	examine
argue	clothing	exercise
around	collect	expect
attempt	color	family
attention	comfortable	flower
awful	company	foreign
awkward	condition	friend
balance	conversation **60**	garden

weather	atmospheric conditions
whether	if it happens that; in case; if

Because of the threatening *weather,* it's not certain *whether* or not the game will be played.

Fill in the blanks: The _____ today is glorious, but I don't know _____ the water is warm enough for swimming.

Write sentences using *weather* and *whether.*

_____

_____

whose	belonging to whom
who's	shortened form for *who is* and *who has*

The man *who's* the author of the latest diet book is a man *whose* ability to cash in on the latest craze is well known.

Fill in the blanks: Rashad is determined to find out _____ van is in the street and _____ been watching him from it with binoculars.

Write sentences using *whose* and *who's.*

_____

_____

| your | belonging to you |
| you're | shortened form of *you are* |

Since *your* family has a history of heart disease, *you're* the kind of person who should take extra health precautions.

Fill in the blanks: When _____ always the last person chosen for a team, _____ self-confidence dwindles away.

Write sentences using *your* and *you're.*

_____

_____

Other Words Frequently Confused

Following is a list of other words that people frequently confuse. Complete the activities for each set of words, and check off and study the ones that give you trouble.

Commonly Confused Words

a	among	desert	learn
an	between	dessert	teach
accept	beside	does	loose
except	besides	dose	lose
advice	can	fewer	quiet
advise	may	less	quite
affect	clothes	former	though
effect	cloths	latter	thought

does	form of the verb *do*
dose	an amount of medicine

Elena *does* not realize that a *dose* of brandy is not the best medicine for the flu.

Fill in the blanks: _____ she understand the importance of taking only the prescribed _____?

Write sentences using *does* and *dose.*

_____

_____

fewer	used with things that can be counted
less	refers to amount, value, or degree

I missed *fewer* classes than Rafael, but I wrote *less* effectively than he did.

Fill in the blanks: I've had _____ attacks of nerves since I began drinking _____ coffee.

Write sentences using *fewer* and *less.*

_____

_____

former	**refers to the first of two items named**
latter	**refers to the second of two items named**

I turned down both the service station job and the shipping clerk job; the *former* involved irregular hours and the *latter* offered very low pay.

Fill in the blanks: Howard doesn't like babies or dogs: the _____ cry when they see him, and the _____ try to bite him.

Write sentences using *former* and *latter*.

_____

_____

TIP Be sure to distinguish *latter* from *later* (meaning *after some time*).

---

learn	**to gain knowledge**
teach	**to give knowledge**

After Roz *learns* the new dance, she is going to *teach* it to me.

Fill in the blanks: My dog is very smart; in just minutes she can _____ any new trick I _____ her.

Write sentences using *learn* and *teach*.

_____

_____

| loose | not fastened; not tight-fitting |
| lose | misplace; fail to win |

I am afraid I'll *lose* my ring: it's too *loose* on my finger.

Fill in the blanks: Lola said to Anthony, "You look dumpy when you wear a

_____ -fitting shirt. You _____ all the wonderful

lines of your chest."

Write sentences using *loose* and *lose.*

_____

_____

| quiet | peaceful |
| quite | entirely; really; rather |

After a busy day, the children were still not *quiet,* and their parents were *quite*
tired.

Fill in the blanks: My friends regarded Ramon as _____ a catch,

but he was just too _____ for me.

Write sentences using *quiet* and *quite.*

_____

_____

| though | despite the fact that |
| thought | past tense of *think* |

Though I enjoyed the dance, I *thought* the cover charge of $5 was too high.

Fill in the blanks: _____ Celeste can now sing in public, she once

_____ she'd never be able to do so.

Write sentences using *though* and *thought*.

_____

_____

Incorrect Word Forms

Following is a list of incorrect word forms that people sometimes use in their writing. Complete the activities for each word, and check off and study the words that give you trouble.

Incorrect Word Forms

being that	could of	would of
can't hardly	must of	irregardless
couldn't hardly	should of	

| being that | Incorrect! Use *because* or *since*. |

because
I'm going to bed now ~~being that~~ I must get up early tomorrow.

Correct the following sentences.

1. Being that she's a year older than I am, Mary thinks she can run my life.
2. I think school will be canceled, being that the bus drivers are on strike.
3. Being that I didn't finish the paper, I didn't go to class.

Effective Word Choice **MASTERY TEST 4**

The following sentences include examples of wordiness. Rewrite the sentences in the space provided, omitting needless words.

1. In my opinion, I think that all people, men and women both, should be treated exactly alike.

   _____

   _____

2. The exercises that Susan does every day of the week give her more energy with which to deal with everyday life.

   _____

   _____

3. I hereby wish to inform you in this letter that I will not be renewing my lease for the apartment.

   _____

   _____

4. All American citizens should consider it their duty to go out and vote on the day that has been scheduled to be Election Day every year.

   _____

   _____

5. In view of the fact that miracle drugs exist in our science today, our lifetimes will be extended longer than our grandparents'.

   _____

   _____

PART 3

Reinforcement of the Skills

Introduction

To reinforce the sentence skills presented in Part Two, this part of the book—Part Three—provides combined mastery tests, editing and proofreading tests, and combined editing tests. The *combined mastery tests* will strengthen your understanding of important related skills. *Editing and proofreading tests* offer practice in finding and correcting one kind of error in a brief passage. *Combined editing tests* then offer similar practice—except that each contains a variety of mistakes. Five of these tests feature "real world" documents—résumés, cover letters, and a job application—so you can apply your skills to situations you are likely to encounter outside the classroom. The tests in Part Three will help you become a skilled editor and proofreader. All too often, students can correct mistakes in practice sentences but are unable to do so in their own writing. You must learn to look carefully for sentence-skills errors and to make close checking a habit.

Whatever your circumstances, someone at some time in your life has helped you. Perhaps you received medical care or temporary housing after a natural disaster such as a hurricane, flood, or forest fire. Perhaps a supportive and caring relative, friend, or teacher took the time to talk with you when you were troubled or had to make a major decision. Take some time to write an e-mail to the person (or persons) who have helped you the most in your life and thank them for their support during difficult times. Be sure to proofread your e-mail for sentence-skills mistakes, using what you've learned from this book.

Combined Mastery Tests

Can you find the sentence-skills errors in the two signs above? On a separate piece of paper, rewrite each sign so that it is grammatically correct. Would you pay less attention to a sign that is confusing or grammatically incorrect? Why or why not?

SCORE
Number Correct

_____ x 5

_____ %

Pronouns **COMBINED MASTERY TEST 1**

Choose the sentence in each pair that uses pronouns correctly. Then write the letter of that sentence in the space provided at the left.

_____ 1. a. When I took my stepson to the California Redwood Forest, he was amazed at how tall they were.

b. When I took my stepson to the California Redwood Forest, he was amazed at how tall the trees were.

_____ 2. a. You can't play the new software on the iMac because it's defective.

b. You can't play the new software on the iMac because the software is defective.

_____ 3. a. Each player on the women's softball team felt proud about her performance in the championship game.

b. Each player on the women's softball team felt proud about their performance in the championship game.

_____ 4. a. I've learned a lot about biking from Eddie, who is a much better biker than me.

b. I've learned a lot about biking from Eddie, who is a much better biker than I.

_____ 5. a. I wanted to browse through the store, but in every department a salesperson came up and asked to help you.

b. I wanted to browse through the store, but in every department a salesperson came up and asked to help me.

NAME: _____

DATE: _____

Pronouns

In the spaces provided, write *PE* for each of the nine sentences that contain pronoun errors. Write *C* for the sentence that uses pronouns correctly. Then cross out each pronoun error and write the correction above it.

_____ 1. Diane received in the mail an ad that said you could make $1,000 a month addressing envelopes.

_____ 2. We refereed the game ourselfs, for no officials were available.

_____ 3. Before any more time is wasted, you and me must have a serious talk.

_____ 4. One of the Boy Scouts left some live embers burning in his campfire.

_____ 5. Everyone who works in the company must have their chest X-rayed every two years.

_____ 6. The instructor gave Mei-Su and I a warning look.

_____ 7. Gina wanted to run in for some bread and milk, but it was so crowded that she decided not to bother.

_____ 8. If them eggs have a bad smell, throw them away.

_____ 9. When I visited a friend at the hospital, you had to pay two dollars just to use the parking lot.

_____ 10. Trevor called Franco at work to say that his father had won the lottery.

NAME: _____

DATE: _____

Faulty Modifiers and Parallelism

In the spaces at the left, indicate whether each sentence contains a misplaced modifier (*MM*), a dangling modifier (*DM*), or faulty parallelism (*FP*). Then correct the error in the space under the sentence.

_____ 1. My parents like to visit auctions, eat Mexican food, and watching horror movies.

_____

_____ 2. An old wreck of wars past, Admiral Hawkeye inspected the ship.

_____

_____ 3. I notified the police that my house had been burglarized by phone.

_____

_____ 4. Dulled by Novocaine, the dentist pulled my tooth.

_____

_____ 5. With sweaty hands and a voice that trembled, Alice read her paper aloud.

_____

_____ 6. At the age of six, my mother bought me a chemistry set.

_____

_____ 7. Cut and infected, Reggie took his dog to the vet.

_____

_____ 8. My neighbor mowed the lawn perspiring heavily.

_____

_____ 9. Midori decided to start a garden while preparing dinner.

_____

_____ 10. To earn extra money, Terry types term papers and is working at the Point Diner.

_____

NAME: _____

DATE: _____

Faulty Modifiers and Parallelism

In the spaces at the left, indicate whether each sentence contains a misplaced modifier (*MM*), a dangling modifier (*DM*), or faulty parallelism (*FP*). Then correct the error in the space under the sentence.

_____ 1. By studying harder, Barry's grades improved.

_____

_____ 2. We put the food back in the knapsack that we had not eaten.

_____

_____ 3. My doctor advised extra sleep, nourishing food, and that I should exercise regularly.

_____

_____ 4. Smelling up the room, I quickly put the trout in the freezer.

_____

_____ 5. Buying a foreign car will cause more family arguments for me than to buy an American car.

_____

_____ 6. Marty is the guy carrying packages with curly brown hair.

_____

_____ 7. My hopes for retirement are good health, having plenty of money, and beautiful companions.

_____

_____ 8. Filled with cigarette butts and used tea bags, I washed the disgusting cups.

_____

_____ 9. I asked Sylvain to dance with me nervously.

_____

_____ 10. Frightened by the rising crime rate, an alarm system was installed in the house.

_____

Passage B

¹If at all possible, try to take you're summer vacation any time accept during the summer. ²First, by scheduling your vacation at another time of the year, you will avoid the crowds. ³You will not have to fight the traffic around resort areas or drive passed dozens of motels with "No Vacancy" signs. ⁴Beaches and campsites will be quite, to. ⁵By vacationing out of season, you will also see many areas at there most beautiful, without the bother of summer's heat, thunderstorms, and insects. ⁶Weather you go in spring or fall, you can travel by car without feeling stuck to your seat or to exhausted to explore the city or park. ⁷Finally, an off-season trip can save you money. ⁸Before and after the summer, prices at resorts drop, for fewer people are demanding reservations. ⁹Its possible to stay too weeks for the price of one; or you might stay in a luxury hotel you might not otherwise be able to afford.

Sentences with commonly confused words (write down the number of a sentence twice if it contains two commonly confused words):

_____   _____   _____   _____   _____

_____   _____   _____   _____   _____

Combined Editing Tests

Psychologists have concluded that there are significant differences in being an only, oldest, middle, or youngest child. Which of these are you, and how did it influence the way you were brought up? Jot down the advantages and disadvantages that come to mind. Use the most important ideas on your list to develop a paragraph on how you think your position in your family affected you.

Fill in each blank with the appropriate personal pronoun.

1. André feeds his pet lizard every day before school. _____ also gives _____ flies in the afternoon.

2. The reporter interviewed the striking workers. _____ told _____ about their demand for higher wages and longer breaks.

3. Students should save all returned tests. _____ should also keep _____ review sheets.

4. The pilot announced that we would fly through some air pockets. _____ said that we should be past _____ soon.

5. Adolfo returned the calculator to Sheila last Friday. But Sheila insists that _____ never got _____ back.

There are several types of pronouns. For convenient reference, they are described briefly in the box below.

Types of Pronouns

Personal pronouns can act in a sentence as subjects, objects, or possessives.

Singular:	**I, me, my, mine, you, your, yours, he, him, his, she, her, hers, it, its**
Plural:	**we, us, our, ours, you, your, yours, they, them, their, theirs**

Relative pronouns refer to someone or something already mentioned in the sentence.

who, whose, whom, which, that

Interrogative pronouns are used to ask questions.

who, whose, whom, which, what

Demonstrative pronouns are used to point out particular persons or things.

this, that, these, those

Note: Do not use *them* (as in *them* shoes), *this here, that there, these here,* or *those there* to point out.

continued

Reflexive pronouns are those that end in *-self* or *-selves*. A reflexive pronoun is used as the object of a verb (as in *Cary cut **herself***) or the object of a preposition (as in *Jack sent a birthday card to **himself***) when the subject of the verb is the same as the object.

    Singular: **myself, yourself, himself, herself, itself**

    Plural: **ourselves, yourselves, themselves**

Intensive pronouns have exactly the same forms as reflexive pronouns. The difference is in how they are used. Intensive pronouns are used to add emphasis. (*I **myself** will need to read the contract before I sign it.*)

Indefinite pronouns do not refer to a particular person or thing.

        each, either, everyone, nothing, both, several, all, any, most, none

Reciprocal pronouns express shared actions or feelings.

        each other, one another

For more information on pronouns, see "Pronoun Types," pages 216–230.

Verbs

Every complete sentence must contain at least one verb. There are two types of verbs: action verbs and linking verbs.

Action Verbs

An *action verb* tells what is being done in a sentence. For example, look at the following sentences:

    Mr. Jensen *swatted* at the bee with his hand.

    Rainwater *poured* into the storm sewer.

    The children *chanted* the words to the song.

In these sentences, the verbs are *swatted, poured,* and *chanted.* These words are all action verbs; they tell what is happening in each sentence.

For more about action verbs, see "Subjects and Verbs," pages 68–70.

Insert an appropriate word in each blank. That word will be an action verb; it will tell what is happening in the sentence.

Practice

4

1. The surgeon _____ through the first layer of skin.

2. The animals in the cage _____ all day.

3. An elderly woman on the street _____ me for directions.

4. The boy next door _____ our lawn every other week.

5. Our instructor _____ our papers over the weekend.

Linking Verbs

Some verbs are *linking verbs*. These verbs link (or join) a noun to something that is said about it. For example, look at the following sentence:

> The clouds *are* steel-gray.

In this sentence, *are* is a linking verb. It joins the noun *clouds* to words that describe it: *steel-gray*.

Other common linking verbs include *am, is, was, were, look, feel, sound, appear, seem,* and *become.* For more about linking verbs, see "Subjects and Verbs," pages 68–70.

In each blank, insert one of the following linking verbs: *am, feel, is, look, were.* Use each linking verb once.

Practice

5

1. The important papers _____ in a desk drawer.

2. I _____ anxious to get my test back.

3. The bananas _____ ripe.

4. The grocery store _____ open until 11 P.M.

5. Whenever I _____ angry, I go off by myself to calm down.

Helping Verbs

Sometimes the verb of a sentence consists of more than one word. In these cases, the main verb will be joined by one or more *helping verbs.* Look at the following sentence:

> The basketball team *will be leaving* for the game at six o'clock.

In this sentence, the main verb is *leaving.* The helping verbs are *will* and *be.*

Other helping verbs include *do, has, have, may, would, can, must, could,* and *should.* For more information about helping verbs, see "Subjects and Verbs," pages 71–72, and "Irregular Verbs," pages 156–170.

Practice

6

In each blank, insert one of the following helping verbs: *does, must, should, could, has been*. Use each helping verb once.

1. You _____ start writing your paper this weekend.

2. The victim _____ describe her attacker in great detail.

3. You _____ rinse the dishes before putting them into the dishwasher.

4. My neighbor _____ arrested for drunk driving.

5. The bus driver _____ not make any extra stops.

Prepositions

A *preposition* is a word that connects a noun or a pronoun to another word in the sentence. For example, look at the following sentence:

A man *in* the bus was snoring loudly.

In is a preposition. It connects the noun *bus* to *man*. Here is a list of common prepositions:

Prepositions				
about	before	down	like	to
above	behind	during	of	toward
across	below	except	off	under
after	beneath	for	on	up
among	beside	from	over	with
around	between	in	since	without
at	by	into	through	

The noun or pronoun that a preposition connects to another word in the sentence is called the *object* of the preposition. A group of words beginning with a preposition and ending with its object is called a *prepositional phrase*. The words *in the bus*, for example, are a prepositional phrase.

Here are some examples of the order of adjectives:

an exciting new movie

the petite young Irish woman

my favorite Chinese restaurant

Greta's long brown leather coat

In general, use no more than two or three adjectives after the article or other noun marker. Numerous adjectives in a series can be awkward: *that comfortable big old green velvet* couch.

Using the Present and Past Participles as Adjectives

The present participle ends in *-ing*. Past participles of regular verbs end in *-ed* or *-d;* a list of the past participles of many common irregular verbs appears on pages 157–160. Both types of participles may be used as adjectives. A participle used as an adjective may come before the word it describes:

There was a **frowning** *security guard.*

A participle used as an adjective may also follow a linking verb and describe the subject of the sentence:

The *security guard* was **frowning**.

While both present and past participles of a particular verb may be used as adjectives, their meanings differ. Use the present participle to describe whoever or whatever causes a feeling:

a **disappointing** *date*

(The date *caused* the disappointment.)

Use the past participle to describe whoever or whatever experiences the feeling:

the **disappointed** *neighbor*

(The neighbor *is* disappointed.)

Here are two more sentences that illustrate the differing meanings of present and past participles.

The waiter was **irritating**.

The diners were **irritated**.

(The waiter caused the irritation; the diners experienced the irritation.)

Following are pairs of present and past participles with similar distinctions.

annoying / annoyed	exhausting / exhausted
boring / bored	fascinating / fascinated
confusing / confused	tiring / tired
depressing / depressed	surprising / surprised
exciting / excited	

Practice

3

Underline the correct word or wording in parentheses.

1. Under my desk at work I keep a (black square little, little square black) heater.

2. The thieves took a (beautiful antique sapphire, beautiful sapphire antique) necklace.

3. The birthday party was held in a (terrific new Mexican, Mexican new terrific) restaurant.

4. Children who are (bored, boring) can get into all kinds of mischief.

5. Larry enjoys life in the country, but his wife finds it too quiet and (bored, boring).

Prepositions Used for Time and Place

The use of a preposition in English is often not based on the preposition's common meaning, and there are many exceptions to general rules. As a result, the correct use of prepositions must be learned gradually through experience. Following is a chart showing how three of the most common prepositions are used in some customary references to time and place:

Use of *On*, *In*, and *At* to Refer to Time and Place

Time

On *a specific day:* on Wednesday, on January 11, on Halloween

In *a part of a day:* in the morning, in the daytime (but *at* night)

In *a month or a year:* in October, in 1776

In *a period of time:* in a second, in a few days, in a little while

At *a specific time:* at 11 P.M., at midnight, at sunset, at lunchtime

Place

On *a surface:* on the shelf, on the sidewalk, on the roof

In *a place that is enclosed:* in the bathroom, in the closet, in the drawer

At *a specific location:* at the restaurant, at the zoo, at the school

Underline the correct preposition in parentheses.

1. I drink coffee only (in, at) the morning.

2. The class will begin (on, at) 8 A.M.

3. Kate needs a baby-sitter (on, at) Tuesday night.

4. There is some fruit (in, at) the refrigerator.

5. (At, In) just one hour, my cousin will be here.

Practice

4

Review Test

Underline the correct word or words in parentheses.

1. We have (room, rooms) for one more passenger in the car.

2. (Is, There is) no need for you to be so angry.

3. Nancy was (embarrassing, embarrassed) when she suddenly forgot her teacher's name.

4. Giving a wrong answer in front of the whole class is (embarrassing, embarrassed).

5. The old dog spends most of its time sleeping on an (old brown ugly, ugly old brown) chair.

6. I feel like (to stay home, staying home) tonight.

7. My girlfriend (understands, is understanding) me very well.

8. We'll look forward to seeing you (on, at) Friday night.

9. The loud (thunder, thunders) made it difficult to talk.

10. I promise (calling, to call) when I get back in town.

Sentence-Skills Diagnostic Test

Part 1

This diagnostic test will help check your knowledge of a number of sentence skills. In each item below, certain words are underlined. Write *X* in the answer space if you think a mistake appears at the underlined part. Write *C* in the answer space if you think the underlined part is correct.

The headings within the text ("Fragments," "Run-Ons," and so on) will give you clues to the mistakes to look for. However, you do not have to understand the heading to find a mistake. What you are checking is your own sense of effective written English.

Fragments

_____ 1. After I had done fifty push-ups. I felt like a worn-out rubber band. I wasn't planning to move until the middle of next week.

_____ 2. My little brother loves to go out at night, especially when the moon is full. My sister is convinced he's a werewolf.

_____ 3. Shelly stood on tiptoe and craned her neck. Trying to see over the heads of the people in front of her. Finally she decided to go home and watch the parade on television.

_____ 4. Janet was excited about the job interview. She decided to have her hair done. And bought a new briefcase so she would look like an executive.

Run-Ons

_____ 5. The instructor assigned two chapters of the book, he also handed out a library research project.

_____ 6. Something was obviously bothering Martha a small muscle in her temple was throbbing.

Part 2 (Optional)

Do the following at your instructor's request. This second part of the test will provide more detailed information about skills you need to know. On separate paper, number and correct all the items you have marked with an *X*. For example, suppose you had marked the word groups below with an *X*. (Note that these examples were not taken from the actual test.)

4. When I picked up the tire. Something in my back snapped. I could not stand up straight as a result.

7. The phone started ringing, then the doorbell sounded as well.

15. Marks goal is to save enough money to get married next year.

29. Without checking the rearview mirror the driver pulled out into the passing lane.

Here is how you should write your corrections on a separate sheet of paper:

4. When I picked up the tire, something in my back snapped.

7. The phone started ringing, and then the doorbell sounded as well.

15. Mark's

29. mirror, the driver

There are more than forty corrections to make in all.

Answers to Introductory Activities and Practice Exercises in Part Two

This answer key can help you teach yourself. Use it to find out why you got some answers wrong—you want to uncover a weak spot in your understanding of a given skill. By using the answer key in an honest and thoughtful way, you will master each skill and prepare yourself for many tests in this book that have no answer key.

SUBJECTS AND VERBS

Introductory Activity *(page 66)*

Answers will vary.

Practice 1 *(68)*

1. I ate
2. Alligators swim
3. April failed
4. movie ended
5. Keiko borrowed
6. children stared
7. newspaper tumbled
8. Lola starts
9. job limits
10. windstorm blew

Practice 2 *(69)*

1. sister is
2. chips are
3. defendant appeared
4. Art became
5. ride . . . seems
6. building was
7. weeks . . . were
8. banana split . . . cake . . . look
9. Jane . . . feels
10. rooms . . . seem

Practice 3 *(69)*

1. clock runs
2. player . . . is
3. shoppers filled
4. trucks rumbled
5. children drew
6. picture fell
7. Chipmunks live
8. uncle monopolized
9. tomatoes were
10. company canceled

Practice 4 *(70)*

1. For that course, you need three different books.
2. The key to the front door slipped from my hand into a puddle.
3. The checkout lines at the supermarket moved very slowly.
4. With his son, Jamal walked to the playground.
5. No quarrel between good friends lasts for a very long time.
6. In one weekend, Martha planted a large vegetable garden in her backyard.
7. Either of my brothers is a reliable worker.
8. The drawer of the bureau sticks on rainy days.
9. During the movie, several people walked out in protest.
10. At a single sitting, my brother reads five or more comic books.

Practice 5 (72)

1. He has been sleeping
2. foundations . . . were attacked
3. I have not washed
4. instructor had not warned
5. bus will be leaving
6. You should not try
7. They have just been married
8. He could make
9. Kim has decided
10. employees should have warned

Practice 6 (73)

1. hypnotist locked . . . and sawed
2. Trina began . . . and finished
3. Nissans, Toyotas, and Hondas glittered
4. Tony added . . . and got
5. car sputtered, stalled, and . . . started
6. Whiteflies, mites, and aphids infected
7. Rosa disconnected . . . and carried
8. We walked . . . and bought
9. Tony and Lola looked . . . and . . . bought
10. aunt and uncle married, . . . divorced, . . . and . . . remarried

FRAGMENTS

Introductory Activity (79)

1. verb
2. subject
3. subject . . . verb
4. thought

Practice 1 (83)

Answers will vary.

Practice 2 (83)

NOTE: The underlined part shows the fragment (or that part of the original fragment not changed during correction).

1. Although the air conditioner was working, I still felt warm in the room.
2. When Drew got into his car this morning, he discovered that he had left the car windows open. The seats and rug were soaked, since it had rained overnight.
3. After cutting fish at the restaurant all day, Jenny smelled like a cat food factory.

4. Franco raked out the soggy leaves that were at the bottom of the cement fishpond. When two bullfrogs jumped out at him, he dropped the rake and ran.
5. Because he had eaten and drunk too much, he had to leave the party early. His stomach was like a volcano that was ready to erupt.

Practice 3 (86)

1. Eli lay in bed after the alarm rang, wishing that he had one million dollars.
2. Investigating the strange, mournful cries in his neighbor's yard, George found a puppy tangled in its leash.
3. As a result, being late for class. *Correction:* As a result, I was late for class.

Practice 4 (86)

Rewritten versions may vary.

1. Glistening with dew, the gigantic web hung between the branches of the tree.
2. Kevin loves his new puppy, claiming that the little dog is his best friend. *Or:* Kevin loves his new puppy. He claims that the little dog is his best friend.
3. Noah picked through the box of chocolates, removing the kinds he didn't like. *Or:* He removed the kinds he didn't like.
4. The grass I was walking on suddenly became squishy because I had hiked into a marsh of some kind. *Or:* The reason was that I had hiked into a marsh of some kind.
5. Steve drove quickly to the bank to cash his paycheck. *Or:* He had to cash his paycheck.

Practice 5 (88)

1. For example, managing to cut his hand while crumbling a bar of shredded wheat. *Correction:* For example, he managed . . .
2. All day, people complained about missing parts, rude salespeople, and errors on bills.
3. For example, using club soda on stains. *Correction:* For example, she suggests using . . .

Practice 6 (89)

Rewritten versions may vary.

1. My little boy is constantly into mischief, such as tearing the labels off all the cans in the cupboard.
2. For example, a hand-carved mantel and a mahogany banister. *Correction:* For example, it had . . .
3. For instance, chewing with his mouth open. *Correction:* For instance, he chewed . . .

4. A half hour later, there were several explosions, with potatoes splattering all over the walls of the oven. *Or:* Potatoes splattered all over the walls of the oven.

5. Janet looked forward to seeing former classmates at the high school reunion, including the football player she had a wild crush on.

Practice 7 *(90)*

Rewritten answers may vary.

1. Fred went to the refrigerator to get milk for his breakfast cereal and discovered about one tablespoon of milk left in the carton. *Or:* He discovered about one tablespoon of milk left in the carton.

2. Then noticed the "Out of Order" sign taped over the coin slot. *Correction:* Then I noticed . . .

3. Our neighborhood's most eligible bachelor got married this weekend but did not invite us to the wedding. *Or:* But he did not invite us to the wedding.

4. Also, was constantly criticizing Larry's choice of friends. *Correction:* Also, he was constantly . . .

5. Wanda stared at the blank page in desperation and decided that the first sentence of a paper is always the hardest to write. *Or:* And she decided that the first sentence of a paper is always the hardest to write.

RUN-ONS

Introductory Activity *(103)*

1. period
2. but
3. semicolon
4. Although

Practice 1 *(106)*

1. down. He
2. station. A
3. panicked. The
4. exam. The
5. wood. One
6. hand. Guests
7. earth. Earthworms
8. party. A
9. time. Her
10. stacks. The

Practice 2 *(107)*

1. class. His
2. increasing. Every
3. properly. We
4. it. Half
5. places. Our
6. water. This
7. speeding. He
8. times. Nobody
9. names. For
10. victory. His

Practice 3 *(107)*

Answers will vary.

Practice 4 *(109)*

1. , and
2. , for
3. , but
4. , for
5. , for
6. , but
7. , and
8. , so
9. , but
10. , so

Practice 5 *(110)*

Answers will vary.

Practice 6 *(111)*

1. service; the
2. *American Idol;* the
3. cool; everyone
4. year; an
5. stop; he

Practice 7 *(112)*

Answers may vary.

1. insecticide; otherwise, the
2. props; also, I (*or* in addition *or* moreover *or* furthermore)
3. basement; instead, he
4. week; consequently, I (*or* as a result *or* thus *or* therefore)
5. semester; in addition, she (*or* also *or* moreover *or* furthermore)

Practice 8 *(112)*

1. seat; however,
2. match; as a result,
3. headache; furthermore,
4. razors; consequently
5. hair; nevertheless,

Practice 9 *(113)*

Answers may vary.

1. because
2. When
3. While *or* When
4. After *or* When
5. before

Practice 10 *(114)*

1. Because (*or* Since) Sharon didn't understand the instructor's point, she asked him to repeat it.
2. Although (*or* Even though) Marco remembered to get the hamburger, he forgot to get the hamburger rolls.

3. After Michael gulped two cups of strong coffee, his heart started to flutter.
4. When a car sped around the corner, it sprayed slush all over the pedestrians.
5. Although (*or* Even though) Lola loved the rose cashmere sweater, she had nothing to wear with it.

SENTENCE VARIETY I

The Simple Sentence
Practice 1 (126)
Answers will vary.

The Compound Sentence
Practice 2 (127)
Answers may vary; possible answers are given.

1. My cold grew worse, so I decided to see a doctor.
2. My uncle always ignores me, but my aunt gives me kisses and presents.
3. We played softball in the afternoon, and we went to a movie in the evening.
4. I invited Rico to sleep overnight, but he wanted to go home.
5. Police raided the club, for they had gotten a tip about illegal drugs for sale.

Practice 3 (128)
Answers will vary.

The Complex Sentence
Practice 4 (129)
Answers may vary; possible answers are given.

1. When the instructor announced the quiz, the class groaned.
2. Because Gene could not fit any more groceries into his cart, he decided to go to the checkout counter.
3. If your car is out of commission, you should take it to Otto's Transmission.
4. After I received a raise at work, I called my boss to say thank you.
5. Since we owned four cats and a dog, no one would rent us an apartment.

Practice 5 (130)
Answers may vary; possible answers are given.

1. Although Ruth turned on the large window fan, the room remained hot.

2. Since the plumber repaired the water heater, we can take showers again.
3. After I washed the sheets and towels, I scrubbed the bathroom floor.
4. You should go to a doctor because your chest cold may get worse.
5. When the fish tank broke, guppies were flopping all over the carpet.

Practice 6 (131)
Answers may vary; possible answers are given.

1. The magazine article that made me very angry was about abortion.
2. The woodshed, which I built myself, has collapsed.
3. The power drill that I bought at half price is missing.
4. Rita Haber, who is our mayor, was indicted for bribery.
5. The chicken pies that we ate contained dangerous preservatives.

Practice 7 (132)
Answers will vary.

The Compound-Complex Sentence
Practice 8 (132)

1. Because . . . and
2. When . . . so
3. Although . . . and
4. Since . . . for
5. If . . . or

Practice 9 (133)
Answers will vary.

Review of Coordination and Subordination
Practice 10 (133)
Answers will vary. Many other combinations are possible.

1. After Louise used a dandruff shampoo, she still had dandruff, so she decided to see a dermatologist.
2. Omar's parents want him to be a doctor, but Omar wants to be a salesman. He impresses people with his charm.
3. While the instructor conducted a discussion period, Jack sat at his desk with his head down. He did not want the instructor to call on him, for he had not read the assignment.
4. When Lola wanted to get a quick lunch at the cafeteria, all the sandwiches were gone, so she had to settle for a cup of yogurt.

5. As I was leaving to do some shopping in town, I asked my son to water the back lawn. He seemed agreeable, but when I returned three hours later, the lawn had not been watered.

6. Because I had eaten too quickly, my stomach became upset. It felt like a war combat zone, so I took two Alka-Seltzer tablets.

7. Vanessa, who enjoys growing things, is always buying plants and flower seeds, but not many things grow well for her. She doesn't know why.

8. My car was struck from behind yesterday when I slowed suddenly for a red light. The driver of the truck behind me slammed on his brakes, but he didn't quite stop in time.

9. Ed, who desperately needed a job, skimmed through the help-wanted ads, but nothing was there for him. He would have to sell his car, for he could no longer keep up the payments.

10. Since the meat loaf didn't taste right and the mashed potatoes had too much salt in them, we sent out for a pizza. It was delivered late, and it was cold.

STANDARD ENGLISH VERBS

Introductory Activity (143)

played . . . plays
hoped . . . hopes
juggled . . . juggles

1. past time . . . -ed or –d
2. present time . . . -s

Practice 1 (145)

1. hates
2. messes
3. feels
4. covers
5. smells
6. C
7. blurs
8. thinks
9. pretends
10. seems

Practice 2 (146)

Charlotte behaves rudely whenever she speaks on her cell phone. First of all, she answers the phone anytime it rings, even at a restaurant or the movies. Then she raises her voice and acts as if the caller is sitting right next to her. Sometimes she waves her hands or laughs loudly. She never notices how people roll their eyes at her. She even asks others near her to be quiet while she talks. If she keeps this up, no one will go anywhere with her–unless she leaves the phone at home.

Practice 3 (147)

1. raced
2. glowed
3. walked
4. sighted
5. stared
6. decided
7. C
8. needed
9. scattered
10. Decided

Practice 4 (147)

Bill's boss shouted at Bill. Feeling bad, Bill went home and cursed his wife. Then his wife screamed at their son. Angry himself, the son went out and cruelly teased a little girl who lived next door until she wailed. Bad feelings were passed on as one person wounded the next with ugly words. No one managed to break the vicious circle.

Practice 5 (149)

1. has
2. does
3. is
4. are
5. was . . . had
6. was
7. did . . . was
8. were
9. had
10. am

Practice 6 (150)

1. ~~be~~ is
2. ~~is~~ are
3. ~~has~~ have
4. ~~don't~~ doesn't
5. ~~is~~ are
6. ~~have~~ had
7. ~~done~~ did
8. ~~have~~ had
9. ~~has~~ had
10. ~~was~~ were

Practice 7 (150)

My mother sings alto in our church choir. She has to go to choir practice every Friday night and is expected to know all the music. If she does not know her part, the other choir members do things like glare at her and are likely to make nasty comments, she says. Last weekend, my mother had houseguests and did not have time to learn all the notes. The music was very difficult, and she thought the other people were going to make fun of her. But they were very understanding when she told them she had laryngitis and couldn't make a sound.

IRREGULAR VERBS

Introductory Activity (156)

1. R . . . screamed . . . screamed
2. I . . . wrote . . . written
3. I . . . stole . . . stolen
4. R . . . asked . . . asked

5. R . . . kissed . . . kissed
6. I . . . chose . . . chosen
7. I . . . rode . . . ridden
8. R . . . chewed . . . chewed
9. I . . . thought . . . thought
10. R . . . danced . . . danced

Practice 1 (160)

1. ~~ate~~ eaten
2. ~~done~~ did (*or* had done)
3. ~~wore~~ worn
4. ~~wrote~~ written
5. ~~gived~~ gave
6. ~~be~~ was
7. ~~broke~~ broken
8. ~~lended~~ lent
9. ~~seen~~ saw
10. ~~knewed~~ knew

Practice 2 (160)

1. (a) sees
   (b) saw
   (c) seen
2. (a) chooses
   (b) chose
   (c) chosen
3. (a) takes
   (b) took
   (c) taken
4. (a) speaks
   (b) spoke
   (c) spoken
5. (a) swims
   (b) swam
   (c) swum
6. (a) drives
   (b) drove
   (c) driven
7. (a) wears
   (b) wore
   (c) worn
8. (a) blows
   (b) blew
   (c) blown
9. (a) begins
   (b) began
   (c) begun
10. (a) goes
    (b) went
    (c) gone

Practice 3 (163)

1. lays
2. lay
3. Lying
4. laid
5. lay

Practice 4 (164)

1. sit
2. setting
3. set
4. sat
5. set

Practice 5 (165)

1. rise
2. raise
3. risen
4. raised
5. rises

SUBJECT-VERB AGREEMENT

Introductory Activity (171)

Correct: The results of the election are very surprising

Correct: There were many complaints about the violent TV show.

Correct: Everybody usually gathers at the waterfront on the Fourth of July.

1. results . . . complaints
2. singular . . . singular

Practice 1 (173)

1. stain ~~on the sheets~~ comes
2. coat, ~~along with two pairs of pants~~, sells
3. roots ~~of the apple tree~~ are
4. sisters, ~~who wanted to be at his surprise party~~, were
5. albums ~~in the attic~~ belong
6. cost ~~of personal calls made on office telephones~~ is
7. cups ~~of coffee in the morning~~ do
8. moon ~~as well as some stars~~ is
9. wiring ~~in the apartment~~ is
10. Chapter 4 ~~of the psychology book, along with six weeks of class notes~~, is

Practice 2 (174)

1. are lines
2. were dogs
3. were dozens
4. are pretzels
5. were Janet and Maureen
6. are rats
7. were boys
8. is house
9. were fans
10. lies pastry

Practice 3 (175)

1. hopes
2. dances
3. deserves
4. were
5. appears
6. offers

7. owns
8. has
9. thinks
10. has

Practice 4 *(175)*
1. match
2. have
3. are
4. plan
5. are

Practice 5 *(176)*
1. were
2. stumble
3. blares
4. give
5. appears

CONSISTENT VERB TENSE

Introductory Activity *(186)*
Mistakes in verb tense: Alex discovers . . . calls a . . .
present . . . past

Practice 1 *(187)*
1. causes
2. decided
3. picked
4. hopes
5. informs
6. sprinkled
7. discovered
8. asked
9. overcharges
10. swallowed

ADDITIONAL INFORMATION ABOUT VERBS

Practice 1 *(Verb Tense; 194)*
1. had walked
2. was feeling
3. had placed
4. was trying
5. is growing
6. had looked
7. has studied
8. has seen
9. was watching
10. had thrown

Practice 2 *(Verbals; 196)*
1. P
2. G
3. G
4. I
5. I
6. P
7. P
8. I
9. P
10. G

Practice 3 *(Active and Passive Verbs; 197)*
1. Eliza organized the surprise party.
2. The comedian offended many people.
3. The neighbors pay for the old woman's groceries.
4. The boys knocked the horse chestnuts off the trees.
5. The exorcist drove the devil out of Regan.
6. Four perspiring men loaded the huge moving van.
7. The inexperienced waiter dropped a tray of glasses.
8. My forgetful Aunt Agatha is always losing umbrellas.
9. Barry Bonds finally broke Babe Ruth's home run record.
10. The airport security staff found a bomb in the suitcase.

PRONOUN REFERENCE, AGREEMENT, AND POINT OF VIEW

Introductory Activity *(201)*
1. b
2. b
3. b

Practice 1 *(203)*
NOTE: The practice sentences could be rewritten to have meanings other than the ones indicated below.

1. Mario insisted that it was Harry's turn to drive.
   Or: Mario insisted to Harry, "It's my turn to drive."
2. I failed two of my courses last semester because the instructors graded unfairly.
3. Don's parents were very much pleased with the accounting job Don was offered.
   Or: The accounting job Don was offered pleased his parents very much.
4. Tony became very upset when he questioned the mechanic.
   Or: The mechanic became very upset when Tony questioned him.
5. I was very nervous about the unexpected biology exam.
6. Paul told his younger brother, "The dog chewed your new running shoes."
7. My cousin is an astrologer, but I don't believe in astrology.
8. When Liz was promoted, she told Elaine.
   Or: Liz told Elaine, "You have been promoted."
9. Whenever I start enjoying a new television show, the network takes it off the air.
10. When the center fielder heard the crack of the bat, he raced toward the fence but was unable to catch the ball.

Practice 2 (205)

1. they . . . their
2. it
3. them
4. it
5. they

Practice 3 (207)

1. his
2. her
3. his
4. his
5. her
6. his
7. her
8. she
9. its
10. his

Practice 4 (208)

1. I always feel hungry
2. they have finished
3. they work
4. we can never be sure
5. she should register
6. he or she should check
   Or: If people plan . . . they should check
7. I do not get paid for all the holidays I should
   Or: One does not get paid . . . one should
8. you should take action
9. we had
10. we want it

PRONOUN TYPES

Introductory Activity (216)

Correct sentences:
Ali and I enrolled in a computer course.
The police officer pointed to my sister and me.
Lola prefers men who take pride in their bodies.
The players are confident that the league championship
   is theirs.
Those concert tickets are too expensive.
Our parents should spend some money on themselves
   for a change.

Practice 1 (219)

1. her *(O)*
2. I *(S)*
3. they *(arrived* is understood) *(S)*
4. her *(O)*
5. she *(S)*
6. he *(S)*
7. She *(S)*
8. We *(S)*
9. I *(am* is understood) *(S)*
10. She and I *(S)*

Practice 2 (220)

Answers will vary. Below are some possibilities.

1. me
2. me *or* him
3. him
4. me *or* her *or* him *or* them
5. me *or* her *or* him
6. I *or* he *or* she
7. I *or* he *or* she
8. them
9. him *or* her *or* them
10. us

Practice 3 (222)

1. who
2. that
3. who
4. whom
5. who

Practice 4 (222)

Answers will vary.

Practice 5 (223)

1. its
2. his
3. mine
4. their
5. ours

Practice 6 (224)

1. That dog
2. This fingernail
3. Those girls
4. those shopping bags
5. that corner house

Practice 7 (225)

Answers will vary.

Practice 8 (226)

1. himself
2. themselves
3. yourself (or yourselves)
4. themselves
5. ourselves

ADJECTIVES AND ADVERBS

Introductory Activity (231)

Answers will vary for 1–4.

adjective . . . adverb . . . *ly* . . . *er* . . . *est*

Practice 1 (234)

1. kinder . . . kindest
2. more ambitious . . . most ambitious
3. more generous . . . most generous
4. finer . . . finest
5. more likable . . . most likable

Practice 2 (234)

1. most comfortable
2. most difficult
3. easiest
4. less
5. best
6. longest
7. most memorable
8. more experienced . . . most experienced
9. worse . . . worst
10. better

Practice 3 (235)

1. violently
2. quickly
3. angrily
4. considerable
5. gently
6. really
7. regularly . . . regular
8. quietly . . . angrily
9. carefully . . . exact
10. Slowly . . . surely

Practice 4 (236)

1. well
2. good
3. well
4. well
5. well

MISPLACED MODIFIERS

Introductory Activity (240)

1. Intended: The farmers were wearing masks.
   Unintended: The apple trees were wearing masks.
2. Intended: The woman had a terminal disease.
   Unintended: The faith healer had a terminal disease.

Practice 1 (241)

NOTE: In each of the corrections below, the underlined part shows what was a misplaced modifier.

1. Driving around in their car, they finally found a Laundromat.
2. In the library, I read that Madame C. J. Walker was the first female African American millionaire.
   Or: I read in the library that Madame C. J. Walker was the first female African American millionaire.
3. Taking the elevator, Evelyn was thinking about her lost chemistry book.
4. Sira chose one of her short stories filled with suspense to submit to the writing contest.
   Or: For the writing contest, Sira chose to submit one of her short stories filled with suspense.
5. Howard worked almost twenty hours overtime to pay some overdue bills.
6. Tickets have gone on sale in the college bookstore for next week's championship game.
   Or: In the college bookstore, tickets have gone on sale for next week's championship game.
7. I returned the orange socks that my uncle gave me to the department store.
8. Looking through the binoculars, the camper saw the black bear.
9. I earned nearly two hundred dollars last week.
10. In the refrigerator, mushrooms should be stored enclosed in a paper bag.

Practice 2 (243)

1. In our science class, we agreed to go out to dinner tonight.
   Or: We agreed in our science class to go out to dinner tonight.
2. On a rainy day in June, Bob and I decided to get married.
   Or: Bob and I, on a rainy day in June, decided to get married.
3. Weighed down with heavy packages, Suki decided to hail a taxi.
   Or: Suki, weighed down with heavy packages, decided to hail a taxi.
4. Without success, I've looked everywhere for an instruction book on how to play the guitar.
   Or: I've looked everywhere without success for an instruction book on how to play the guitar.
5. Over the phone, Mother told me to wash the car.
   Or: Mother told me over the phone to wash the car.

7. tubes: simple plural meaning more than one inner tube

   rivers: river's, meaning "rushing currents of the river"

   currents: simple plural meaning more than one current

8. directors: director's, meaning "specialty of the director"

   films: simple plural meaning more than one film

   vampires: simple plural meaning more than one vampire

9. copies: simple plural meaning more than one copy

   company's: company's, meaning "tax returns of the company"

   returns: simple plural meaning more than one return

   years: simple plural meaning more than one year

10. Scientists: simple plural meaning more than one scientist

    Africa's: Africa's, meaning "Congo region of Africa"

    relatives: simple plural meaning more than one relative

    dinosaurs: simple plural meaning more than one dinosaur

Apostrophe with Plural Words Ending in -s
Practice 9 (329)

1. firefighters'
2. drivers'
3. friends'
4. grandparents'
5. soldiers'

QUOTATION MARKS

Introductory Activity (338)

1. Quotation marks set off the exact words of a speaker.
2. Commas and periods following quotations go inside quotation marks.

Practice 1 (340)

1. "Have more trust in me," Lola said to her mother.
2. The instructor asked Sharon, "Why are your eyes closed?"
3. Christ said, "I come that you may have life, and have it more abundantly."
4. "I refuse to wear those itchy wool pants!" Ralph shouted at his parents.
5. His father replied, "We should give all the clothes you never wear to the Salvation Army."

6. The nervous boy whispered hoarsely over the telephone, "Is Linda home?"
7. "When I was ten," Lola said, "I spent my entire summer playing Monopoly."
8. Tony said, "When I was ten, I spent my whole summer playing basketball."
9. The critic wrote about the play, "It runs the gamut of emotions from A to B."
10. "The best way to tell if a mushroom is poisonous," the doctor solemnly explained, "is if you find it in the stomach of a dead person."

Practice 2 (341)

1. Greg said, "I'm going with you."
2. "Everyone passed the test," the instructor informed the class.
3. My parents asked, "Where were you?"
4. "I hate that commercial," he muttered.
5. "If you don't leave soon," he warned, "you'll be late for work."

Practice 3 (341)

Answers will vary.

Indirect Quotations
Practice 4 (342)

2. Lynn replied, "I thought you were going to write them this year."
3. Eric said, "Writing invitations is a woman's job."
4. Lynn exclaimed, "You're crazy!"
5. Eric replied, "You have much better handwriting than I do."

Practice 5 (343)

1. He said that as the plane went higher, his heart sank lower.
2. The designer said that shag rugs are back in style.
3. The foreman asked Susan if she had ever operated a lift truck.
4. My new neighbor asked if I would like to come over for coffee.
5. Mei Lin complained that she married a man who eats Tweeties cereal for breakfast.

Practice 6 (344)

1. The young couple opened their brand-new copy of Cooking Made Easy to the chapter titled "Meat Loaf Magic."

2. Annabelle borrowed Hawthorne's novel The Scarlet Letter from the library because she thought it was about a varsity athlete.

3. Did you know that the musical West Side Story is actually a modern version of Shakespeare's tragedy Romeo and Juliet?

4. I used to think that Richard Connell's short story "The Most Dangerous Game" was the scariest piece of suspense fiction in existence–until I began reading Bram Stoker's classic novel Dracula.

5. Every year at Easter, we watch a movie such as The Robe on television.

6. During the past year, Time featured an article on DNA titled "Building Blocks of the Future."

7. My father still remembers the way that Sarah Brightman sang "Think of Me" in the original Broadway production of The Phantom of the Opera.

8. As I stood in the supermarket checkout line, I read a feature story in the National Enquirer titled "Mother Gives Birth to Alien Baby."

9. My favorite song by Aretha Franklin is the classic "Respect," which has been included on the CD Aretha's Best.

10. Absentmindedly munching a Dorito, Hana opened the latest issue of Newsweek to its cover story, "The Junk Food Explosion."

COMMA

Introductory Activity (354)

1. a
2. b
3. c
4. d
5. e
6. f

Practice 1 (356)

1. red, white, and blue
2. laundry, helped clean the apartment, waxed the car, and watched
3. patties, special sauce, lettuce, cheese, pickles, and onions

Practice 2 (356)

1. Cold eggs, burnt bacon, and watery orange juice are the reasons I've never returned to that diner for breakfast.
2. Andy relaxes by reading Donald Duck, Archie, and Bugs Bunny comic books.
3. Tonight I've got to work at the restaurant for three hours, finish writing a paper, and study for an exam.

Practice 3 (357)

1. When I didn't get my paycheck at work, . . . According to the office computer,
2. After seeing the accident, . . . Even so,
3. To get her hair done, . . . Once there, . . . Also,

Practice 4 (357)

1. Even though Tina had an upset stomach, she went bowling with her husband.
2. Looking back over the last ten years, I can see several decisions I made that really changed my life.
3. Instead of going with my family to the mall, I decided to relax at home and to call up some friends.

Practice 5 (359)

1. deadline, the absolute final deadline,
2. cow, a weird creature, . . . dish, who must also have been strange,
3. Tod, voted the most likely to succeed in our high school graduating class, . . . King Kongs, a local motorcycle gang,

Practice 6 (359)

1. My sister's cat, which she got from the animal shelter, woke her when her apartment caught fire.
2. A bulging biology textbook, its pages stuffed with notes and handouts, lay on the path to the college parking lot.
3. A baked potato, with its crispy skin and soft inside, rates as one of my all-time favorite foods.

Practice 7 (360)

1. C
2. mountain, and
3. eating, but
4. speech, and
5. C
6. car, but
7. C
8. shops, but
9. C
10. math, for

Practice 8 (361)

1. fries," said Lola. . . . She asked, "What
2. Coke," responded Tony.
3. grief," said Lola. . . . "In fact," she continued, "how much

Practice 9 (361)

1. "You better hurry," Thelma's mother warned, "or you're going to miss the last bus of the morning."

2. "It really worries me," said Marty, "that you haven't seen a doctor about that strange swelling under your arm."
3. The student sighed in frustration and then raised his hand. "My computer has crashed again," he called out to the instructor.

Practice 10 (362)

1. sorry, sir,
2. 6, 1954,
3. June 30, 2010,
4. Seas, P.O. Box 760, El Paso, TX 79972
5. Leo, get

Practice 11 (363)

1. When I arrived to help with the moving, Jerome said to me that the work was already done.
2. After the flour and milk have been mixed, eggs must be added to the recipe.
3. Because my sister is allergic to cat fur and dust, our family does not own a cat or have any dust-catching drapes or rugs.
4. The guys on the corner asked, "Have you ever taken karate lessons?"
5. As the heavy Caterpillar tractor rumbled up the street, our house windows rattled.
6. Las Vegas, Miami Beach, San Diego, and Atlantic City are the four places she has worked as a bartender.
7. Thomas Farley, the handsome young man who just took off his trousers, is an escaped mental patient.
8. Hal wanted to go to medical school, but he does not have the money and was not offered a scholarship.
9. Joyce reads a lot of fiction, but I prefer stories that really happened.
10. Because Mary is single, her married friends do not invite her to their parties.

OTHER PUNCTUATION MARKS

Introductory Activity (373)

1. list: eggs
2. life-size
3. (1856–1939)
4. track;
5. breathing—but alive.

Practice 1 (374)

1. work:
2. Sears:
3. Hazlitt:

Practice 2 (375)

1. death; in . . . death; and
2. ridiculous; for example,
3. National Bank; Jay . . . State Bank; and

Practice 3 (376)

1. condition—except
2. minutes—in fact,
3. work—these

Practice 4 (377)

1. sixty-five dollars . . . sixty-five cents
2. ten-year-old . . . self-confident
3. split-level

Practice 5 (377)

1. charts (pages 16–20) in
2. prepare (1) a daily list of things to do and (2) a weekly study schedule.
3. drinkers (five or more cups a day) suffer

DICTIONARY USE

Introductory Activity (381)

1. fortutious (fortuitous)
2. hi/er/o/glyph/ics
3. be
4. oc/to/ge/nar'/i/an
5. (1) Identifying mark on the ear of a domestic animal
   (2) Identifying feature or characteristic

Answers to the activities are in your dictionary. Check with your instructor if you have any problems.

SPELLING IMPROVEMENT

Introductory Activity (393)

Misspellings:
akward . . . exercize . . . buisness . . . worried . . . shamful . . . begining . . . partys . . . sandwichs . . . heros

Practice 1 (396)

1. studied
2. advising
3. carries
4. stopping
5. terrified
6. compelled
7. retiring
8. hungrily
9. expelling
10. judges

Practice 2 *(397)*

1. groceries
2. towns
3. policies
4. bodies
5. lotteries
6. passes
7. tragedies
8. watches
9. suits
10. bosses

OMITTED WORDS AND LETTERS

Introductory Activity *(404)*

bottles . . . in the supermarket . . . like a windup toy . . .
his arms . . . an alert shopper . . . with the crying

Practice 1 *(405)*

1. When I began eating the box of chicken I bought
   at the fast-food restaurant, I found several pieces
   that consisted of a lot of crust covering nothing but
   chicken bones.
2. Gwen had an instructor who tried to light a piece of
   chalk, thinking it was a cigarette.
3. In his dream, Ray committed the perfect crime:
   he killed his enemy with an icicle, so the murder
   weapon was never found.
4. Dr. Yutzer told me not to worry about the sore on
   my foot, but I decided to get a second opinion.
5. As the little girl ate the vanilla sugar cone, ice
   cream dripped out of a hole at the bottom onto her
   pants.
6. When thick black clouds began to form and we felt
   several drops of rain, we knew the picnic would be
   canceled.
7. After spending most of her salary on a new computer,
   Suki hasn't left her room for days.
8. As butter melted on the stove, I assembled the
   ingredients for a pie.
9. Keith put the pair of wet socks in the oven, for he
   wanted to dry them out quickly.
10. Because the weather got hot and stayed hot for
    weeks, my flower garden started to look like a
    dried flower arrangement.

Practice 2 *(406)*

1. boyfriends . . . blows
2. curses
3. paragraphs . . . events
4. windshields . . . cars
5. houses . . . highways
6. days . . . times
7. billboards
8. chairs . . . pillows
9. watchtowers . . . states
10. motorists . . . trucks

Practice 3 *(407)*

Answers will vary.

COMMONLY CONFUSED WORDS

Introductory Activity *(411)*

1. Incorrect: your
   Correct: you're
2. Incorrect: who's
   Correct: whose
3. Incorrect: there
   Correct: their
4. Incorrect: to
   Correct: too
5. Incorrect: Its
   Correct: It's

Homonyms *(412–422)*

Sentences will vary.

all ready . . . already
brake . . . break
coarse . . . course
here . . . hear
hole . . . whole
it's . . . its
knew . . . new
no . . . know
pear . . . pair
past . . . passed
piece . . . peace
plain . . . plane
principal . . . principle
write . . . right
then . . . than
there . . . their . . . they're
through . . . threw
to . . . two . . . too . . . too
wear . . . where
weather . . . whether
whose . . . who's
you're . . . your

Index